Making it WERK

A dancer's guide to the business of professional dance

Michelle Loucadoux
Shelli Margheritis

II

Table of Contents

Foreword VII

Introduction 1

1. Getting Started 6

2. Never Stop Learning 17

3. Networking 32

4. Branding 51

5. Representation 60

6. Unions 77

7. Auditioning 93

8. Working 106

9. Thriving 133

10. Transitioning 148

Afterword 154

Acknowledgments 158

To my loving parents, Kay and Dan Lookadoo, who taught me the importance of diligence and hard work. And more importantly, how to be a good human.

Foreword

As a working dancer from the age of twelve, the dance industry has been the most prominent and consistent environment I have known. The dance and entertainment industry is always evolving, therefore artists considering dancing as a career will need to be flexible in their physical agility as well as in their pursuit of opportunities.

Moving from being a performer to being an agent for choreographers, educators and dancers has allowed me to view the industry from both the artist's and business person's perspectives. As an advocate to the industry for the betterment of artist conditions, I have found a sense of responsibility to educate dancers on how to make opportunity meet responsibility. It takes a team to produce a project, and that team will rely on an artist to not only have the skills to be hired, but also to have an education, a good reputation, steely dedication, focus, and commitment.

To anyone pursuing a dream as an artist, I will say to be grateful for the creative gift that lies within you. I also encourage all artists to continue educating themselves artistically, to know their dance history, push their boundaries creatively, define how to network, and to clearly understand the business perspective of the industry. When an artist has a level head and integrity, the entertainment industry can bring a lifetime of fulfillment. When an artist applies their talent and knowledge effectively, they raise the bar of excellence within the industry, therefore continuing the evolution of the creative spirit within the Arts.

-Shelli Margheritis
Los Angeles, 2017

Introduction

  I was not the best dancer in the world. Not even remotely. I made a living dancing for 13 years in five Broadway shows, four ballet companies, and innumerable films, commercials, and music videos, but I can tell you with 100% confidence that it was NOT because of my turnout, my perfect physique, or my innate artist's pedigree.

  I had been genetically granted with a solid 140-degree turnout, a 65% accuracy rate on my triple pirouettes (only to the right), and a very pronounced pear shape that one very callous ballet teacher referred to as my "tutu butt." I was not exactly Sylvie Guillem, to say the least. I also did not enter the world as the prodigy of some well-known actor, dancer, music artist, athlete, or producer. I was part of an epically supportive, very kind, middle-class North Carolinian family who had all made their honest livings doing most everything OTHER than the arts. There were no baby photo shoots of myself swaddled in Chanel on the cover of US magazine, no private coaching sessions with Jerome Robbins, and definitely no teenage red carpet premieres. In short, when I entered the industry, much like the majority of all dancers in the world, I did not enter with any kind of significant advantage.

  I was, though, a hard worker, a good performer, and (what I believe to have been most influential in my career), a savvy businessperson. I showed up early, I kept in touch, I branded myself correctly, I researched ahead of time; I budgeted my time, my energy, and my money, and I made a lot of industry connections. And I mean a LOT of industry connections. Like, thousands and THOUSANDS of industry connections. Why? Because creating personal connections with individuals gets you significantly more jobs than perfect dance technique. My theory was and still is: the less natural ability you have, the more personal industry connections you should make. If you hear people say that the dance industry is all about who you know, they're telling the truth. Conquering the dance industry IS all about who you know. But that adage is not the complete truth. Who you know is very important, but what's even more important is WHAT those "people you know" know about you.

AND continued success in the dance industry is also contingent on making sure that IF people know you and they know good things about you, that they'll remember you.

One of my favorite sayings is, "There's a reason they call it 'show business,' not 'show play'." The entertainment industry is, in fact, very much business, but many dancers fail to master or even acknowledge that fact. Even the most talented dancers will struggle to create a career with any kind of longevity if they don't learn how to be savvy businesspeople as well as skilled artists and technicians. Whether it's the world of company dance, commercial dance, or Broadway dance, a dancer must know how to market themselves, how to approach and cultivate business relationships, how to find and choose auditions, how to conduct themselves on set, how to manage politics backstage, how to strategically seek out choreographers, and so on. The list of "business" elements that dancers should employ in their careers is as lengthy as the number of terms in a Vaganova ballet class. And, unfortunately, those business elements are often disregarded.

The hard truth is that most dance careers are a hodge-podge of different "gigs". Unlike corporate America, dance rarely offers a defined career path to success. Dancers don't leave college and go from an internship to an associate position to, say, an engineering position, to a project engineer, to an engineering manager, and finally work their way up to an engineering director; the whole time, garnering appropriately increasing salaries and benefits. Some of the more prominent dance companies do offer longer-term steady work with the opportunity for advancement and job security, but salaries are generally fairly low and positions in companies are few and very difficult to acquire. Even contracted company dancers often have to seek out supplemental dancing or teaching gigs during lay offs and breaks to stay afloat.

Outside of company work, commercial dance and Broadway dance jobs can also be very competitive, usually requiring an audition or multiple auditions to be offered each position of employment. And most of these jobs last less than one year. In fact, many dance jobs last less than one week. To a layperson, this career path might seem impossible (and undesirable), but the point of this book to say that IT'S NOT! A career in dance is both attainable and artistically, financially, and physically rewarding if you know exactly how to make it work.

    The secret to a lasting career in the dance industry is to put all of the pieces together. Most dancers think of each "gig" as an individual entity. By shifting a dancer's focus to conquering the industry as a whole (rather than just booking the next gig), a dancer sets himself or herself up for an increasing likelihood that they will be the first to be hired when a new job presents itself. In short, dancers should play the "long game". When dancers make an effort to consistently cultivate and maintain relationships with their agents, managers, choreographers, producers, directors, and other dancers, they are more likely to work more consistently. Likewise, if dancers know how to properly market themselves, creating consistent and flattering (but not annoying) social media presences, digital marketing packages, and correspondence plans, they put themselves in the best possible position to succeed. Even more, just plain making friends and fans and keeping in touch makes a significant difference in a dancer's employment portfolio. The more information or skills a dancer can acquire, the more marketable they make themselves when their friends and fans are privy to their varied talents. Obviously, this sounds like a lot to worry about in addition to just dancing, but it's not. And it's pretty easy to create and maintain with a little pre-planning and attention to detail. And a little career versatility.

    There is a vastly accepted misconception that there is only one type of career in the dance world. I can say with full confidence that any idea even remotely resembling that misconception is absolutely incorrect. It's like saying there is only one kind of career in medicine. We all know that pharmacists, pediatricians, pharmaceutical salespersons, neurosurgeons, and registered nurses are not all the same career. And we don't assume that when one takes, for instance, biology, that one must become, say, a pediatrician. Why, then, do we as a society assume that ballet dancers have to dance with a ballet company? Why can't they choreograph for films, teach ballet classes at a university, start a dance therapy practice, produce private ballet-centric events, be a Pilates instructor, coach gymnasts in ballet, design tutus, dance in television commercials, open a dance school, write a ballet blog, or EVEN WRITE BOOKS ABOUT DANCE? Education in the vast amount of dance-centric careers is also part of the putting-the-pieces-together approach to mastering the dance industry. Often, dancers neglect the vast number of possibilities that can come from a life of training in dance and they don't realize that dance performing-adjacent employment can not only supplement, but also enhance their performing careers. And it can double the number of industry connections (and subsequently double the number of potential job opportunities).

Why is the "who you know" so important? The business of dance is less about soutenus than it is about sales. Dancers, in essence, have a product that they're selling. This product has been developed, cultivated, and honed for many years and it is a product that is malleable, versatile, and reusable. Sounds like a great product right? It sure is! Because that product is . . . YOU. As a dancer, the product you're selling is yourself (that sounds WAY worse than it is). When a dancer attends an audition, they hope that a choreographer/director/casting director/producer will hire (or buy) what they're selling – "I'm a great dancer. Hire me!". Hopefully, if that audition goes well, the choreographer/director/casting director/producer decides to "buy the product" and the dancer receives a contract. Seems easy enough, right? Unfortunately, it's not that simple.

Unlike most careers, dancers are not trying to talk a home-buyer into buying a new condo, a hedge fund manager into investing in an IPO, or even a holiday shopper into purchasing a new sweater. When dancers audition for a job, every part of their persona is auditioning –including, but not limited to, their physicality, artistry, reputation, and personality. While most dancers think they're "selling" just their technique, the real truth of the matter is that they're selling their technique AS WELL AS their "look", their versatility, their ability to creatively solve problems, their work ethic, their special skills, their personality, their ability to work well with others, their experience, their fan base, and their loyalty. While that seems like a lot of factors to manage, most dancers that master even some of them end up with long and profitable careers while dancers that focus solely on technique and neglect the other parts of "the business" generally have a significantly lower long-term success rate.

If you're a young dancer looking to enter the industry or an experienced dancer looking to get more jobs, why not take every opportunity to be as successful as you can be? Learning to navigate the dance industry is one of the best things you can do to further or start your professional dance career. Should you continue to go to class as much as possible to hone and improve your technique? Absolutely. I am not, in any way, saying that dancers should allocate any less of their resources to time inside the dance studio. All "business" advice aside, the more time spent learning, practicing, and rehearsing, the better the dancer. Hands down, perfecting good technique in dance class is where every successful dance career starts. There is no amount of networking that can make a dancer with poor technique a success. But, if you have done the work at the barre, you should know that there is a lot more to learn. This book is about how to get a leg up (pun intended) **outside** the dance studio, how to be an active participant in molding a successful career in dance, and how to . . . Make it WERK.

1

Getting Started

Everyone has to start somewhere. Sometimes when dancers graduate from high school or college and step into the industry, they can feel like they're on a deserted island with no idea how to start their careers. And truth be told, entering the dance industry can be very similar to being marooned in the middle of nowhere. So, let's imagine that you were actually dropped on a random uninhabited beach and forced to survive with only a big bag full of supplies. What would you do first? Look for water? Start to build a shelter? OR . . . Would you first take a moment to look at exactly what is in your bag of supplies? Rule number one of getting started in the dance industry: take inventory. Do you have a rope? A machete? Flint? What do you know and have that can help you survive and how can you use it?

Whether you like it or not, you have to start your career with the skills and assets that you already have. Don't worry, though, chances are, you have more resources than you think. And you may not know it, but the skills and assets you already possess can probably be used in more ways than one. The moral of the story is: you never know what you have until you look in the bag.

SKILLS

The obvious first thing to do when entering the dance industry is to take an inventory of your skill set. Yes, you can dance. (Or maybe you can't, but chances are, if you're reading this book, you probably can.) The question is, HOW can you dance? Are you brilliant at ballet? Are you super skilled at spinning on your head? Do you pop more eloquently than Marie Poppins? Great! All of that will be useful. Now, think outside of the box.

Make a physical list all of your skills. Even the ones you're not so sure should be included. (Yes, physical list. Like, write it down . . . On paper. I know we live in a digital age, but as a dancer, you're likely to be a kinesthetic learner which means that if you physically write things down, you'll be more likely to commit them to memory.) So, maybe you took an Irish step dancing module in college, but don't consider it to be one of your strongest skills. Doesn't matter. Write it down. Or maybe you played the violin in your high school orchestra, but you think it has nothing to do with your first passion, commercial dance. You never know. Write it down. Really - make a list of ALL of your skills. Did your grandma teach you to knit? List it. Do you have random interests like gardening and playing video games? These can be good additions to your list. JUST WRITE THEM ALL DOWN.

Your list may take you a few days or a few weeks to complete and that's completely fine. Chances are, a lot of things will pop up after you have finished your list that you suddenly realize are skills. Cool. Add them. It's more than likely that your list will continue to grow for the rest of your life as you add skills, hobbies, and even things you've learned while working on dance gigs. More skills = greater marketability = more jobs = more money. Take out the middle bits and more skills = more money. While that's a pretty vast oversimplification, it's pretty accurate on a broad scale. Look at it this way:

In one year, there will be hundreds of auditions in Los Angeles looking for blonde female hip-hop dancers. With that description, it's you and 4,000 people auditioning for the job. All other things being equal, your chances of snagging a place in this specific job are one in 4,000. BUT, what if the audition notice is looking for blonde hip-hop dancers that can tumble? You have to guess that not every blonde hip-hop dancer in Los Angeles can tumble. Not even close, in fact. Let's assume that only 100 of those 4,000 dancers can tumble. Now your odds are significantly better. I'll say that 1 in 100 is WAY better odds than 1 in 4,000.

As dancers, we rarely see the audition notices that go out to agents and managers for submissions, but I have it on pretty good authority that those audition notices get very specific. The more skills you have, the more eligible you are for these specific jobs. (Not to mention, having more fun skills like juggling, tumbling, and bone breaking just makes you a cooler person!) I've actually seen choreographers ADD things to projects because of a dancer's particular skill set. Many moons ago, I performed in a regional theater production of Brigadoon with a fellow dancer who happened to be a pretty mean violin player. Guess what? After the director read her special skills, he decided to make her character play the violin in the show. She not only got to showcase one of her special skills, but she also got to have a more featured role than the other ensemble dancers in the show. Special skill: win!

Incidentally, if you acquire a great new skill, don't forget to tell your representation about it (if you have representation). When those very specific audition notices go out and you haven't let your agent or manager know what you can do, you might as well not have your new skill at all. (Other than for an occasional party trick.) Most agents and managers will have you fill out a special skill sheet when you sign with the agency. These sheets can be a bit daunting because they generally list pretty much every skill in the universe and you have to rate your proficiency in these skills on a scale from one to five. Don't worry. Nobody expects every dancer to know how to do everything. The most important thing to remember is to be HONEST. (There's nothing worse than a dancer rating himself a 4 out of 5 in horseback riding when he hasn't been on a horse since he was six years old. Why? Because when he is offered the music video gig that requires him to ride a horse through a shot, his seemingly white lie will cost the music video production a big chunk of change to recast the role. Just tell the truth, people!)

AGENT'S TAKE: Keep your bag of supplies fresh, up to date, and viable to the current marketplace. Make sure to research those who are making a difference within the dance industry (dancers, choreographers, directors). What do you notice about the people that are being effective in the industry and how can you learn tactics from them to apply to your career goals?

Rome was not built in a day; your career will not be either. Most dancers expect a lot from themselves. Please breathe and give yourself a break. When you start to lay the bricks of your career, remember to allow the concrete to dry so you have a solid and realistic foundation. Continue your training, integrate into the dance community, and then start to network.

The other reason to make a list of your skill set is to have the opportunity to look at yourself objectively as a marketable dancer. Ask your friends in the industry to look at your list of skills and let you know if there's something they think is missing. Maybe you're a great hip-hop dancer with a very "street" look but your pal notices that you have never taken a break dancing class. These skills go really well together and could GET YOU A JOB! Now you know what new skill to focus on attaining. Or say you're an avid runner, you love martial arts, and you are a naturally athletic person. Maybe you should consider stunt school? Add all of those skills together and you get a very marketable commodity in both the dance AND the film industry. And that equals more dollar signs.

Speaking of which, I will always say that the amount of money spent learning a new marketable skill in the world of dance (or performing in general) will always pay off two, three, or ten-fold in the long run in both satisfaction, enjoyment, and . . . jobs. Start with what you have and expand upon it. The fact of the matter is the successful dancer is the one that refuses ever to stop learning.

AGENT'S TAKE: Present the best version of your authentic self. No one knows you better than yourself; therefore it is up to you to make sure all assets you have are acknowledged to expand your opportunities. (Are you interested in aerial work? Do you do gymnastics? Are you a contortionist? Are you interested in expanding your vocal skills?)

Once you recognize the vast areas of skills you have and define them, make sure you inform those who are considering you for their projects and make sure to update your representation as you acquire and expand your skills.

PHYSICALITY

If you want to be a cellist, you drive to the music store and purchase a cello. That cello you purchased is now your instrument. If you want to be a painter, you purchase paint and canvas, create a piece, and then attempt to sell it. That painted canvas is your creation and your paintbrushes are the instruments you used to make your art. As a dancer, your physical body is your instrument and your art is what you can do with it. When you think about it . . . it's a bit limiting. That's one of the rough things about becoming a performing dancer. You can't just buy or purchase another person's body in which to dance like you can a cello or paintbrush. You have what you're born with and that's pretty much it. The fortunate thing, though, is that you as a person have significantly more control and mastery of your instrument than any visual artist or musician because, well, you live in it every day. There is also a degree to which you can shape your body as your instrument, but you're also born with the body in which you're born. Whatever it is, celebrate it. There is a place in the dance industry for pretty much every shape, size, color, style, and gender of dancer (I just heard an agent say, and I quote, "Androgynous is totally in right now"). Your job as a dancer is just to find the right job and stylistic dance fit for your physicality and your passions.

If you have crazy turnout, long thin legs, and super bendy feet and you have never studied ballet, I would consider that a serious missed opportunity. If you are naturally a muscular mesomorph-type person and you have never been to a fitness class or learned to properly lift weights, get in there! The next time your agent calls with an audition for a dance workout video or an athletic company's commercial, you can go in confidently to the audition room and look AND dance the part. The point is, play to your strengths. There may be skills that go very well with your physicality that you haven't explored yet. Cross-reference your skill set with your physicality inventory. Are you part Hawaiian and you've never taken a hula class? Get on it.

Part of this is linked to branding which you'll read about a bit later, but a lot of this is common sense. Really look at what you're working with as a dancer from an outside perspective and try to guess how you would cast yourself. Then work to enhance the skills and physical appearance of whomever that dancer is! Acquire and build the skills that dancer might need in an audition situation. But first, start with what you have. And acknowledge what you have. Again, there is work for everyone in this industry. Knowing WHICH work for which you're most appropriate starts with understanding AND EMBRACING the best version of the physicality you're born with. Your quirks may just be the things that make you stand out of the crowd.

AGENT'S TAKE: Evaluating your physicality is essential. Many people look at their physicality as limiting; however, it is the opposite. Understanding your body type and abilities will allow you to articulate what is unique about you and your personal physicality. Focusing on the positive and what you bring to various opportunities within the industry will allow you to have clarity on your special attributes.

PEOPLE

So, you're just getting started in the industry. (Or not – in which case, feel free to skip to chapter two). You may be a newbie to auditioning or new to a big city, but you inevitably know SOMEONE in the industry. Or you know someone who knows someone. Or you know someone who knows someone who knows someone. It is humanly impossible to have NO connections. You probably have a lot of connections that you don't even know about. So ask! Don't be afraid to ask your friends, family, and teachers to introduce you to people they might know that are affiliated with or in the dance business. Maybe they know someone and maybe they don't, but it can't hurt to ask. And in today's day and age of email and social media, you can make unobtrusive connections quickly and easily just a short introduction. Maybe your hometown hairdresser lived in New York for a few years in his twenties. Ask him! Do you have family near Los Angeles? Maybe they have a friend that has a daughter that's a professional dancer out there. Ask them! It's super important to use all of the resources available to you when you're getting started in the dance industry. People are (and will continue to be) some of your most valuable resources and conduits to a long and successful dance career.

What's the best place to start? Start with your dance teachers. Chances are if a person has taught you some type of dance, they will be willing to endorse your work to people that they know. And there is a pretty huge chance that at some point your teachers did more dancing and less teaching for their livelihood. That means they probably still know folks that can help you out in the industry. Make a list of all of the teachers you have had that instructed or coached or choreographed on you for more than a few weeks and start reaching out and using your resources.

For instance, a fictional gal named Jackie just graduated from college with a BFA in dance and wants to move to New York to be a contemporary dancer. Her ultimate goal is to gain a position in a contemporary dance company and live in the most exciting city in the world, but she's a bit overwhelmed by the options and choices in front of her. Jackie emails her favorite contemporary teacher from college and asks if he knows any dancers/choreographers/agents/casting directors in New York. Nice work, Jackie! First step: taken.

It turns out, Jackie's teacher DOES know a few people in New York. As requested, her college teacher emails a working dancer and an agent and e-introduces Jackie to both of them. Bam! Jackie's door is now open for communication with two huge new contacts in New York. Jackie emails the agent her headshot, resume, and reel along with a request to meet and chat about a future partnership. Then, she sets up a call with the working dancer her teacher recommended to get the "lay of the land" in New York. Jackie then chats with this dancer for a short while, takes notes, and acquires a new friend on social media.

Let's say the agent declines a meeting, but tells Jackie to contact the agency in the future once she gets a little more experience. This is good news. Why you might ask, is rejection good news? Because this agent has now seen Jackie's name and her work. Familiarity is half the battle, and there are few things more exciting to some folks in the industry as "fresh meat." Would it have been better if the agent had signed Jackie right away? Maybe. But not every one of your initial "people-connections" will be an immediate win. Breaking into the industry takes time. (Much like breaking into your coconut on your deserted island once you've gone through your bag of supplies on your survival reality show!)

The dancer Jackie chats with on the phone gives her a few tips as to which classes to take at STEPS, Alvin Ailey, and Broadway Dance Center in New York. "Ginger's contemporary class is a great place to be seen. Ginger is known for hiring dancers for her projects from her open classes and she just started her own company". Bingo! Jackie just received very important insider information AND just made a new friend and contact in the industry (see the chapter on networking). Thanks to ONE of Jackie's teacher's referrals, she now has a toe-hold (pun intended) on her move to New York. Now, multiply these two referrals by the number of contacts that you have. If you contact and gain information from all of your people's connections before even moving to a big city or setting foot in your first dance class as a professional, you will enter the industry with a significant advantage over the majority of your peers.

Be creative in making your list of people to reach out to. Maybe you have a friend who dances for a contemporary company in Phoenix. Or you follow a contemporary dancer in New York's social media that you don't know. Or your mother's friend lives in New York and has nothing to do with the dance world. Reach out anyway. Worst-case scenario, your mom's friend could potentially help you with finding an apartment or a roommate.

AGENT'S TAKE: Make sure to remember that the industry is a community. It is also a target-specific arena of resources. If you do not ask questions about the industry such as who is having an audition, what is the best class to take, etc., then you are limiting yourself to finding the answers yourself. Although the industry seems to be a huge entity, keep in mind that it is a close and connected group of individuals that are dedicated to the business. The industry is seeking talented, smart, ethical, consistent, dedicated, and creative individuals.

Make sure to ask questions to a variety of individuals to get several perspectives. This will help you use the information from many resources to allow you to confidently make the choices that you are best suited for you.

MONEY

Every young dancer I have encountered is always impatient to get their career started. We all get it. Dance careers can be short and they often favor the young. BUT moving to a new city with no monetary savings and no plan of attack can be significantly more detrimental to your career than waiting a few months, teaching a few extra 3-year-old combo dance classes at your local studio, and getting started on the right foot (or the left, depending on the combo).

Consider a dancer named Nick that moves immediately to a

new city after graduating from high school or college (without any savings) and starts auditioning for gigs from the minute he arrives. Great! Consider that this dancer has been given enough money by his parents to pay the security deposit and first month of his rent and decides to get a restaurant job to keep him afloat. Again, great thinking. While restaurant gigs are not so glamorous, once you've established yourself in a restaurant, they can be pretty flexible and could be handy to earn you a bit of extra cash between dancing gigs. Let's also say that this gentleman dancer snags an agent almost immediately. (Don't worry – there's a lot more information on how to snag an agent in chapter 6). AND let's say that Nick also is almost immediately offered a job waiting tables at a nice restaurant. It seems like life is pretty perfect. And it is . . . for a while, anyway.

Then Nick starts getting great dance auditions from his new agent. He's the newbie at his restaurant job, so he's initially scheduled for four lunch shifts per week and can balance the two pretty well for a few weeks. Then he gets a call from his agent to audition for the Broadway revival of Cats (yes, he's one of those rare male dancers that geeks out over wearing a unitard and lurking about in a full face of makeup eight shows per week . . . that and production contract money). But his Cats audition is scheduled during one of his lunch shifts. It's an agent appointment for a very specific replacement, so our guy can't change his audition time. 'No problem,' he thinks. Nick just has to switch shifts with another server. He tries, though, but has no luck (who wants to work a Monday lunch shift at a restaurant in Union Square, anyway?). He asks his restaurant manager for the day off and is informed that if he misses his lunch shift, he will be put on probation (no work = no money) for a week. And he for sure doesn't want to call his agent and turn down the audition. (Incidentally, agents HATE that. Inevitably, they have worked hard to get you that appointment and if you turn it down, it's essentially wasting their time). On top of all of that, his second month's rent is due at the end of the week and if he doesn't have the money from his restaurant job, he will be short. What to do?

AGENT'S TAKE: Representation understands that you need to pay your bills while opportunities are being sought for you. It is best to always communicate with your agent on your

other commitments. They can be far more understanding if you pass on a short term job when you have informed them of your situation. It you don't, you may be perceived as not being committed to your career.

Unfortunately, it's not a question of what Nick should do, it's a question of what he should HAVE DONE. If Nick had had a little money saved, he wouldn't mind being docked a week's pay and would be able to pay the rent with his savings, go to the audition, book it, and quit his restaurant job. Get the point? Good. Let's dance. (Couldn't help the Janet Jackson reference).

My suggestion? When starting out in the dance business, you should have at least three months of living expenses. That's the minimum a dancer should have saved before embarking on their journey toward sweet success in the industry in any big city (New York, Los Angeles, London, Chicago, Tokyo, etc). Six months' living expenses is even better. That means saving for rent, health insurance, car payments, food expenses, phone payments, dance classes, and everything else you might need that costs coin. This may sound excessive, but most financial advisors would suggest that you have six months living expenses saved regardless of your profession. It's even more important to have some dough in your piggy bank in the dance business; a business that is often erratic and where one injury can threaten to halt your income for a long periods of time. Also, when your friends all go to take Fancy Hip Hop Choreographer's class at The Edge, you are not the one to say, "I have to stay home because I need to save money to pay my rent."

The other key side of the coin is to not spend TOO much time saving up before getting out there. If you can't save in your current location, it's better to leap first and doggie paddle than stay outside of the pool for an extended period of time. Again, dance careers can be short. If it's going to take you five years to save six months of expenses, I recommend you just bite the bullet and do that saving in a city where you can at least start to establish some strategic connections.

AGENT'S TAKE: Being a smart dancer means being smart with your finances as well. If finances are not your forte,

ask your fellow dancers if they know someone who is. What is their system, how do they do it? Ask!

~

The idea is that the less time a dancer needs to spend on working to pay for surviving, the more time they have to spend on taking class, making connections, workshopping new pieces with working choreographers, creating quality digital content, and, well, being a dancer. The harder you hit the industry at the beginning, the better for your career. And no choreographer wants to hear, "I actually can't assist you on your audition for the Grammys because I have this Thursday babysitting gig I can't give up." Babysitting is cool, but I'm guessing that if you're reading this, you don't want to do it for a living.

~

AGENT'S TAKE: There is a perception that if you choose to be an artist, you are choosing to be a starving artist. That perception is a false illusion. The magic behind the truth is to be smart with the choices you are making by researching all of the opportunities you are considering. Having the privilege to be creative does not mean you must sacrifice being financially successful; making smart choices is like honing the muscles in your body. Yes, you can be physically and financially fit!

~

In conclusion, you already have a lot of the tools you need to start a successful career in the industry before you even get into it. And when you're starting out, don't be afraid to ask for help. Most humans love giving advice on topics they're passionate about, so help someone help you. It is more than likely that people will be more than willing to advise you on a multitude of subjects . . . and you'll probably make their day in the meantime. Like any good dancer doing a grand jété on a moving cruise ship, look before you leap. Education is everything when starting a career in dance. Being smart about utilizing what you already have to get what you want is the best way to step into the ring and start duking it out with the pros.

2

Never Stop Learning

Technique is important in dance. Always. And GOOD dance technique is mega-important. BUT, there are many things other than spending hours in the dance studio that are valuable in crafting a complete dance career. Some dancers think there will eventually be an "I've gotten there!" moment in their career: a point where they're like, "Yes! Awesome! I'm now a professional dancer, and I can rest and enjoy the fruits of my dance classroom labors." My very vehement response to this notion is . . . NOOOOOOOO! I'm here to say that's the WORST thing a dancer of ANY AGE can think. You have never "made it" and you should for sure never become complacent in anything. Particularly your training. In short, great dancers never stop growing.

A dancer's training NEVER stops. Please forgive all of the shouting capital letters, but this is HUGE - a dancer should NEVER stop learning new things. (For that matter, I think humans should seek to continue to learn new things, no matter what their profession.) You'll read about it all through this book. The more things you know, the more skills you have, the more people you know . . . the more jobs you book. Simple as pie. (Or plié.) The key to obtaining an additional edge over your fellow dancers, though, is strategically using your continued training to further your connections and to increase your marketability.

For categorization and simplicity, I'll divide this chapter into the following categories: 1) Choose your teachers wisely; 2) Act, act, act; 3) Do what you hate; and 4) When in doubt, improvise. Let's get started.

CHOOSE YOUR TEACHERS WISELY

When you graduate from school, enter the professional world of dance, and begin to audition (and subsequently realize that the world of dance is TINY in comparison to most other industries), you should consider your continued education an offshoot of your career. Taking class with influential teachers can be one of the most beneficial things you can do for your future career. There are many reasons for this, but the most important reason is . . . your teacher may be hiring.

Many teachers that offer open classes at venues like Millennium, Broadway Dance Center, STEPS, and The Edge are often also working extensively as choreographers in the industry. Think about it. Teaching an open class is an ideal situation for an experimentally-minded choreographer to have a weekly gaggle of dancers that are proverbial guinea pigs for new choreography. AND the choreographer gets paid to experiment on these enthusiastic dancers. Why WOULDN'T a choreographer want that?

If a choreographer isn't lucky enough to teach a weekly open dance class and is tasked with choreographing, say, a well-known music artist's upcoming international tour, they'll probably want to work out some ideas on live folks (instead of alone in his or her living room). If they do want to do this, the choreographer must pay to rent studio space, gather a group of friends who can dance, and (hopefully, if they're not a cheapskate) pay their dancers for their time. That's a lot of money! The other option is to MAKE money to teach an ongoing open class or two at a reputable venue and generate a profit. Oh, and potentially find new great dancers for their future projects. For the choreographer and the dancer, it's win/win situation.

Rule number one of choosing your teachers wisely is to find working choreographers that teach open classes and TAKE THEM. You never know when these folks will be setting a huge new piece at, say, Choreographer's Carnival and are seeking to employ talented and reliable dancers whose work they know and trust for performances. Chances are when a choreographer gets a gig, they are more than likely to go back to their mental catalog of students from the classes they teach and think, "Who do I know from my class that I can hire to do this gig?". If you've been a regular attendee of their class and you've TALKED to them (dude, just introduce yourself and say hi and that you enjoy their class from time to time), then you've officially entered yourself into the running for any gig that might come up. And you've probably gotten to take great classes in the meanwhile.

Incidentally, and this should go without saying, if you are taking open classes at a very public dance venue in a large city, please show up looking good. You don't have to have professional makeup and a $40 blowout (that would get all sweaty anyway), but if you show up looking crap-tastic in your pajamas, you might involuntarily put yourself out of the running for a potential job. All things being equal, the dancer that looks like they give a hoot about making themselves presentable when going into a public setting. It also never hurts to get someone's attention with your outfit or fun and funky personal style and then seal the deal with your technique. This sounds pretty superficial, right? Maybe it is. But, it is also a reality of the industry. Your look is part of the package you're selling.

The second rule of choosing your teachers wisely is to never underestimate the power of the strategic private lesson. Sometimes, a private lesson with the bad-ass choreographer or casting director is precisely the thing that you need to get you on the "short list" for upcoming gigs. Rightly, this tactic is not a popular favorite of dancers just starting out because it's a very expensive (and slightly ballsy) tactic. BUT, if it works, it can be one of the most effective. Here's how it works:

First off, you should identify your favorite choreographer, casting director, or agent – the one you believe could be the most influential in your career. For instance, let's say you want to be a dancer in a specific Broadway show. That's a great goal. So, do a little research and find the name of the choreographer of this show. Second, find where and when this choreographer teaches and show up for their class and/or workshop (chances are, these folks are teaching a master class or regularly scheduled class somewhere). Third, just take said choreographer's class and be your awesome self. If it's a recurring class, you should make a point of taking it more than once to establish a relationship with this individual. THEN . . .

(Here's the slightly gutsy part). After you've established a working relationship with your new favorite choreographer, approach him or her in a casual manner, compliment his or her work/teaching method/choreography style, etc., and ask him or her if they teach private lessons. Make sure to site WHY you want private lessons from this individual. Perhaps you want to work on picking up choreography quickly, and they teach particularly fast. Perhaps you are a contemporary dancer looking to get a better grasp on your hip hop technique. Whatever it is, make sure it's a legitimate reason and that you DON'T mention ANYTHING about your super secret ulterior motive to be in this choreographer's Broadway show.

Now, the worst thing that can happen is that this choreographer is flattered by the compliment, doesn't have the time, and turns you down. This is NOT BAD! Why? You have now successfully displayed a commitment to furthering your learning (which is respectable in any vocation), and you've made another point of contact with your favorite choreographer, so they'll be more likely to remember you in the future. Again, in most cases, rejection equals (a mild but marked) success. As they say in the PR business, any press is good press. (This is not necessarily true if you're, say, running a dog-fighting ring or if you are arrested for smuggling illegal substances into the country. But if you're just trying to further your craft, you're golden.)

The best thing that can happen is that your favorite choreographer says yes to your private lesson request. You win! Set it up now! Thank him or her, offer up two or three possible meeting times (you should have identified days you're available before asking, so you don't look unprepared), ask your choreographer about the best location or neighborhood to meet, and ask what the choreographer charges for an hour-long lesson. Now, don't be surprised if it's a steep price. If they're a working teacher and choreographer, their time is very valuable. Also, remember that you may have to tack on a studio rental fee for this lesson. Hopefully, though, you have prepared for this ahead of time and are willing to shell out some dough to further your education and your career.

Here's the best part about procuring a private lesson from a working director, casting director, or choreographer. YOU GET THEIR CONTACT INFORMATION! This is something that is and can prove to be very valuable in the long run. It is also something this is very fragile and precarious. Whatever you do, protect your new contact's information with your life and use it sparingly and wisely. Only bother your more-than-likely-very-busy new contact to politely set up or confirm your lessons. Remember, they're probably very busy! And whatever you do, DO NOT dole out this information to ANYONE.

If you've succeeded in setting up your private lesson, then congratulations are in order. You're now a private student of your favorite choreographer/director/casting director. Now, please, pretty please take your lessons very seriously. Always be on time, work hard, confirm ahead of time, take notes, pay them on time, be humble and cooperative, etc. During your time with this teacher, you can give them a great idea of what it would be like to work with you as an employee (hopefully it's a good and positive experience).

After a few lessons with your new contact, you can gently start dropping in little personal details to let him or her know that you're an aspiring/working and currently auditioning dancer (if they didn't already know). "That pirouette correction you gave me worked so well last week when I was at the Chicago audition! Thank you!" Eventually, (hopefully), your choreographer becomes a resource of information and a new addition to your contact list. THEN, when there is an audition for a replacement for the Broadway show that they've choreographed (after you've studied with them for a reasonable amount of time), you can casually mention that you're considering going to the audition and ask if he/she thinks you should go/would be right for the role/if they're truly hiring, etc. It's only not weird if you've established a connection already.

Your choreographer of choice is, in fact, a human being that has feelings, a sense of propriety, and (hopefully) a genuine desire to help other folks out. Once you've established a relationship with him or her, that relationship can turn out to be a great gateway into the industry. It can also provide a great insider voice and opinion from the other side of the table because it's likely that your choreographer wants to help out a fellow hard-working dancer in whatever way they can. Who knows? You may be able to some day do your choreographer/private lesson teacher a favor. (Also, they might be more willing to help you out because they might feel like they owe you a favor since you've shelled out a good amount of dough). Not that people can be bought, but . . .

Agent's Take: Keep in mind that most prominent educators and choreographers do not provide private lessons, however being in front of them and holding their attention is a skill that will put you in the running for potentially working for them. Don't limit or pigeonhole yourself with one educator or choreographer that you connect with; remember to be diverse, so you continue to open doors for yourself.

ACT, ACT, ACT

If you're reading this book, I'm going to guess you're a dancer or a close friend or family member of one. Guess what? If you're a dancer, you're also an actor (or a close friend or family member of one). Dancers ARE actors. Do most dancers have to memorize lines and cry on cue? No. But dancers are asked to genuinely convey emotion with their bodies and their faces rather than with words. That makes them actors. Even further, I will venture to say that dancers need to be even better actors than actor-actors because they are tasked with telling a story WITHOUT words.

From a practical standpoint, I can say with complete confidence that the most technically proficient dancer in an audition rarely gets the job. Do you know who does get the job? The best storyteller. Now, technique is very important. Don't get me wrong. If you can't demonstrate the baseline of technique that will be required to execute the choreography, you won't be in the running regardless of what happens. But, I have been in front of and behind the table for over 20 years (ahem, not to date myself or anything), and the general consensus from behind the table is that any dancer with a basic level of technical proficiency can learn to emulate dance steps. In the words of one of my favorite Broadway producers, "You can teach almost anybody a dance step. You can't teach someone how to have a personality". Every choreographer is looking for dancers with that "extra something." That "star quality." From my standpoint, "star quality" equals . . . ACTING . . . while dancing. More often that not, that's what gets jobs.

Think of all of your favorite and most memorable moments from that competition dance television reality show that shall not be named that we all have probably loved to watch for many years. Which dances do you remember? I'd guess that 90% of the ones that popped into your head were the ones that moved you. They were more than likely dances that moved your heart, not your legs. You probably remember the pieces that told a powerful story. When directors, choreographers, and producers remember dancers from an audition, it works the same way.

How does one become a great actor-dancer? Well, I'd say to start with one of the things about which dancers know more than most average human beings. Muscles. There are 43 muscles in your face. Incidentally, that is more muscles than in both of your legs combined. Most dancers spend decades in a studio training the muscles in their bodies to do things as automatically as possible. For instance, how many times have you done a grand plié in first position? Probably tens of thousands. How many of these pliés have you done with a pleasant expression on your face? Don't know? That's a large part of the problem.

    I cannot stress enough that you should be training the muscles in your face in dance class while you're training the rest of your body. No, this is not acting training, but it will at least keep you from doing an entire audition or performance with, for lack of a better phrase, "resting b*$# face." Remember, people want to hire people that are pleasant to be around and whether your actual personality is pleasant under that "RBF" or not may be something that a choreographer never gets to find out because they will probably cut you from the audition before they get to know you.

    Also, statistically, more people have "RBF" when they're concentrating on a difficult task. (Okay, there aren't actual statistics on that, but I'm pretty confident it's true.) So, PLEASE, relax your face and rehearse smiling, or at least looking pleasant, while you're dancing. And make sure not to employ that creepy smile-with-your-mouth-but-not-your-eyes-possessed-doll-toddlers-and-tiaras smile. That's even worse than "RBF." Save that for Halloween. The act of simply relaxing the muscles in your face is something that most of us dancers aren't used to doing. Let's be honest, relaxing muscles in general is not really our thing. But get this: if you happen to be doing a good job genuinely feeling a specific emotion while you're dancing, this emotion might not come through if your face is super tense. Think of it as wearing a mask. Masks don't move. Or change. If you plaster on a fake visage, your genuine emotions can be knocking behind that mask trying to get out and genuinely effect the world. In short, relaxing your facial muscles is the first step to becoming a better dancer-actor and taking off that mask of tension.

    Second and most obviously, I would highly recommend taking acting classes. I get it; you think you're too busy dancing as it is and you don't want to add one more thing to your class roster. That's understandable, but guess what? You can't afford to NOT take acting classes. Nowadays, dancers are consistently asked to speak (meaning . . . act) in film, television, commercials and the stage. (Thank you for opening up the opportunities, Step Up movies, Glee, and live television musical events!) Why limit the number of job opportunities you might have by not expanding your list of skills to include being able to SPEAK? To me, it's a no-brainer. (You all know what I mean. Yes, most humans can speak, and you're probably one of them, but there is TECHNIQUE to it.) It's not dissimilar to walking. If you're a dancer, there are innumerable ways you can walk across a stage for different situations and, chances are, you've worked very hard to perfect all of them. Most folks that aren't dancers just . . . walk. Like, from one place to another. Steps to a dancer are like words to an actor. Most people in the world (if they're lucky) can talk, but only actors know how to artfully craft their words into any narrative and character at any time. Why, as an artist, would you not want to have that skill? My advice? Find a weekly acting class in your area and get on it.

    I understand - acting can be a very scary thing for dancers. Think about it: dancers often get into dancing in the first place because they feel more comfortable expressing themselves through movement rather than words. On top of this, once a person decides to pursue dance at an advanced level, they spend hours and hours in a dance studio silently dancing while a teacher or choreographer tells them what to do. (Anybody ever get in trouble for talking in ballet class? I sure did.) In general, dancers are taught in the studio to speak only when spoken to, so a verbal expression of thoughts and emotions sometimes becomes even more foreign for dancers than most other humans. The best way to get over any fear of speaking (or exposing genuine emotion while speaking) is to step boldly into the uncomfortable . . . until the uncomfortable becomes comfortable.

    If you've never taken an acting class, you'll be surprised how much you already know about how to act from your dancing. Dancers tell stories (or "act") on stage all the time. And guess what? Dancers are tasked with telling some pretty complex stories in performance with no words. Now, call me crazy, but I would consider this kind of acting significantly harder than acting WITH words! Dancers also inherently know a significant amount about body language and with a little instruction, can successfully physically embody a variety of vastly different characters. They can also subconsciously decipher the body language of fellow actors and respond to it. These are things that take actor-actors years to comprehend and perfect.

Worst-case scenario, you take an acting class and never book a speaking role on any stage or on-camera project ever in your life. But, in this acting class, you've inevitably learned to express yourself more eloquently, you have become more confident in your own spoken word, and you've networked with a new group of people. (You'll more than likely meet a plethora of folks in your acting class that JUST MIGHT need a choreographer, country line dancer, or background waltzer for an upcoming short film that they're producing. Or you might just meet a person or two who might be interested in a private dance lesson. You never know.) Best-case scenario, you're good at acting and you move on to nab a role in a film, a television show, or a role in a musical. GOOD! Call your agent, let them know, show off your new skills, and watch your auditions multiply. Oh, and don't forget to add your new training and skill to your resume.

Still don't think acting pertains to you? Okay, say you're a commercial dancer and you believe in dancing for dancing's sake. You maintain that there is rarely a story behind music video choreography and you think that only artsy-fartsy dancers act while they dance. Well, you're wrong. There's ALWAYS a story. And you should always be acting – even as a commercial dancer. And the more specific the story you create, the more interesting your dancing is. The choreographer does not necessarily need to explicitly tell you which story you are telling. If there's no story, make it up! It will make you a much more interesting dancer, no matter what story you create behind the choreography.

Say, you're at an audition for a music video for Carrie Underwood. The audition calls for "hot cowgirls," and you find yourself kicking and squatting at a dance call alongside hundreds of other women. Guess what? Even if the people behind the table don't explicitly create it, there can be a story behind your cowgirl's steps. While you're learning choreography, your challenge is to create the story you're telling for yourself. It doesn't have to be complex at all! Break it down. Your first clue was in the audition breakdown. "Hot" cowgirls. Your job is to turn "hot" into an action. Maybe it's "entice someone to come home with me" or "show off my assets to make someone jealous". Whatever it is, you can work with that one word "hot" to make your performance exponentially more interesting than your neighbor's. What next?

Okay, let's say you pick "show off my assets to make someone else jealous". Great. Then, choose an imaginary person to whom to show off to and put that imaginary person somewhere at the front of the room near (but not in place of) the folks behind the table. Once you know your choreography, commence "showing off" while you're dancing. For instance, your main objective in dancing is to convince this imaginary person to join you for a drink at a table behind you. Dance the given combination with that motivation and I guarantee it will be much more interesting than simply dancing steps and plastering on a fake smile (or, even worse, RBF). Go, go Gadget acting. That's it. And that, friends, will get you more jobs than crazy flexibility, a perfect body, or astounding tricks any day.

AGENT'S TAKE: Acting skills will help you fully understand the story you aim to project. What are the lyrics of the song? What do they mean? What is your character? How will you project this character with a through line? Having acting skills will enhance how you approach the storyline and how your role is performed.

DO WHAT YOU HATE

Whatever you do, resist the urge to skip this section! I readily admit that the title of this section sounds terrible, but it's not as bad as I'm sure you're imagining. (And also, it's a short section, so even if it's terrible, it will take up very little of your time). This idea of doing what you hate with regard to dance is a huge catalyst for increased diversity of skill and subsequently increased employment opportunities. Human nature dictates that we gravitate toward performing the tasks at which we know we will be successful. So, we keep working on making the things we love to do even better than branching out and trying something new. How many of you are fabulous right pirouetters? If you are, what do you think your one-year right pirouette quantity is compared to your left pirouette quantity? Chances are, it's probably higher. Significantly higher, if you're like most people. But, when you think about it, shouldn't you practice twice as many turns on your bad side to even yourself out?

For example, an accomplished sixteen-year-old ballet dancer

named Sydney is planning to audition for ballet companies after high school. Sydney is a beautifully flexible young lady with uncanny control and a pretty consistent quintuple pirouette (to the right). Great job, Sydney. Sydney, though, hates jazz, modern dance, pirouettes to the left, and anything that involves what she deems as "getting funky". I'm sure you can guess what my advice to Sydney would be. Take jazz! Turn to the left ONLY! Take a weekend adult-level modern class! There are very few ballet companies these days that only do classical repertoire, so the jazz and modern classes will help Sydney when the choreographers get a little funky in her company auditions. The extra non-ballet classes will also help her even more a year later when she has joined a company and they do a repertory show featuring Tharp, Balanchine, and Bill T. Jones. And I don't know any ballet companies that only require their dancers to turn to the right. (I make all of the ballet classes I teach start all of their combinations to the left).

AGENT'S TAKE: Many auditions will make sure that turn sequences, extensions and jetés are requested on both right and left sides to verify the artists' diversity. Don't be a one trick pony.

There are some schools of thought that the new generation of dancers should choose what their strength is, capitalize on it, and create a brand and a career out of it. While I do think that's a good idea, creating a career out of one skill in today's dance industry is virtually impossible. Dance styles have converged in such a way that it is often hard to even name a particular style when watching dance. Tendu, battement, lay out, step pencil turn, step to parallel, do two chest pops and do a knee drop. This kind of dance fusion is no longer revolutionary. It's the norm. The more styles you are comfortable with, the more skills you have, the better equipped you are to attend any audition and show your best self. Remember, most of the time you don't know what the combination is before you arrive at an audition and if you haven't tried a knee drop before in class, you might end up looking a little silly.

One of the many ways dancers excel in life is in their ability to be disciplined. That is when they want to be disciplined. If I had a dollar for every ballet dancer I heard come up with an excuse for not taking a jazz funk class or even a quarter for every hip hop dancer I've heard explaining why tap "isn't their thing", I'd probably be lounging on my yacht drinking a margarita while writing this book. We dancers (and humans) love to do what we like and what we're good at. It truly takes some guts to take a class or embark upon a project that makes us uncomfortable. But, guess what? The more uncomfortable you make yourself, the more comfortable you become.

Agent's take: Pushing yourself as an artist and stepping into new areas that are uncomfortable will not only expand your range, but will clarify what areas you are most drawn to. To grow the most, you will need to consider developing skills that are out of your comfort zone.

The more you diversify your dance education, the more marketable you are and the more useful you are to choreographers that like to mix it up stylistically. This doesn't just apply to dancer-dancers. I know more than a few musical theater dancers that hate to sing. One particular young lady almost always cries when she gets a callback to sing, she always hesitantly sings "All that Jazz" from Chicago, and she pretty much never books the job. She has taken two singing lessons in her LIFE. Why? Because she maintains that she hates singing. (Now, granted, I would venture to tell her that she should perhaps choose another career, but that isn't my place). But, what an easy fix for her career and her confidence if she would just do what she hates? How much more confident would she be if she took weekly singing lessons? Or how much more relaxed would she be if she even committed to going to a weekly karaoke night at a bar with friends where she could belt it out for her inebriated cohorts? Exponentially. And maybe this gal will never book a gig that asks her to sing, but at least she might stop crying in the hallway at invited calls . . .

AGENT'S TAKE: Singing can be incredibly intimidating to dancers, especially as dancers tend to aim for perfection. Breathe and approach vocal lessons with the understanding that

this skill will help you. No one is asking you to be a rock star, but the skills you gain will make you better vocally, assist you in losing the fear of singing, and teach you how to implement breathing techniques that will help you in dance. It's a win-win.

A little disclaimer before we move on: I'm not recommending that you make a habit of doing only what you hate. If gestural contemporary work is your jam, I do not recommend abandoning your favorite contemporary class at The Edge. But, I'm guessing every dancer has a sneaking suspicion that there's an area in their dancing that needs work that they may be neglecting. So, add a class in this genre to your schedule. Be brave! Go for it! Worst-case scenario, you get a little better at whatever it is that you dislike doing and you get to work a few new muscles. Best-case scenario, you begin to like what you hate.

IMPROVISATION

Improvisation is becoming more and more prevalent in the dance industry . . . by the day. It is not uncommon in Los Angeles to walk into a national commercial audition for, say, a popular beverage that is seeking dancers and be asked to improvise your audition. It goes like this: you walk into an empty (probably carpeted) room, the lone casting director turns on a random piece of music, turns on a camera, and then simply says "Slate and then go". That's it. In this kind of (very popular) scenario, most dancers are given somewhere between 20 and 45 seconds to show their stuff and then they're out the door. No choreography, no resume and headshot, no second chance.

Improvising in dance is a skill that every dancer should have. Yes, I'll say it again – improvisation is a skill. So many dancers believe that improvising is a kick, a turn, a jump, and a sensible sassy walk until you're off camera. That kind of improvisation is probably not going to get you the attention of the choreographer or job. If you didn't already know, there's a technique to improvising. And if the choreographer behind the camera knows this, it can be glaringly obvious if you don't. Please, particularly if you consider yourself a commercial dancer and if you have not taken a dance improvisation class, run (don't walk) to the class that's nearest you. If you are one of the lucky dancers who has taken a good amount of dance improvisation classes, I implore you to continue to rehearse and hone your improv skills. They're hugely important! I, personally, have booked three national commercials and a principal dancing role in a feature film just from improvising, No choreography at all.

The other reason to be a great improviser is that some choreographers like to have their dancers start or assist in the creation process alongside them. I worked with a very successful choreographer who one day brought a stack of books with photos of the particular character we were playing into rehearsal. He then told us to take some time looking at the photos and to come up with 16-32 counts of choreography with a partner that embodied the movement quality we got from the characters in the books. If you're not so good at making things up on the fly, this kind of thing can be a daunting task. If you've honed your improvisation and choreography skills, it's likely that something you create will end up in the final choreography of a piece. (Incidentally, this particular choreographer I was working with should not be thought of as any type of lazy or unimaginative. He proceeded to come into the room afterward and craft sections of our choreography into an intricately woven piece of art that is still performed around the world today).

Without going deeply into a lesson on improvisation, I will note that there are a few secrets to getting a choreographer or director's eye if you're improvising in a larger group of people as well. As I've stated before, intention is everything, but there are a few powerful tools that many people neglect to employ when making up dance steps on the fly. I won't go into detail - that's for your local improv teacher to tell you about, but I will say to never underestimate the power of stillness or a purposeful and committed simple walk.

~

AGENT'S TAKE: Improv can make or break an audition for an artist. Make sure your improv is in line with the tone of the project and that your movement connects to the music to which you are asked to improvise. Be aware of your space. And be aware that if you over emphasize movement in trying to grab the attention of casting, you may be doing yourself a disservice. Work to hone your improv skills, so you make smart choices in auditions.

As you might have guessed, the main lesson of this chapter is that you should never stop learning. Ever. The other facet of this, though, is that learning is inherently networking. One of my favorite memes on social media is the phrase, "You have the same number of hours in the day as Lin Manuel Miranda". The vast difference between how people choose to use their 24 hours in a day is astounding. Having said that, there are ONLY 24 hours in a day and a dancer's career can sometimes be relativity short. So, kill two birds with one stone and continue your education in your professional years in a way that will help continue your career as well. Further your contacts, gain skills that will make you more employable, and greatly increase the likelihood that you will book the jobs of your dreams.

3

Networking

We all know that networking is important. In any industry, be it advertising, finance, education, or dance, a relationship (or even an acquaintance with mutual professional respect) between an interviewer and an interview-ee can be the deciding factor in procuring any job. Furthermore, dance is an industry in which interviewing (or auditioning) happens more than **TEN** times as often as many other more traditional professions. I'm pretty sure the world would be a very different place if all other non-performance-based professions interviewed numerous times every month or three months, or even six months, for a new job.

Because of the frequency with which dancers audition, networking in the business of dance could be viewed as ten times more important than it is in most other professions. Sadly, though, many professional dancers don't have any networking strategy other than seeing their pals in dance class and going to the rare performance. In the age of unobtrusive accessibility to practically anyone via email and social media, it is simple to put together a plan to be at the forefront of every casting director and choreographer's minds when they're looking to cast new projects. A little research, a little organization, and a little savvy will yield a LOT of results.

All dancers must be pros at knowing all of the players in their corner of the industry and making sure that those players, large or small, know who they are. While that is a good starting point, "the business" is significantly more complicated than that. Consistent employment in the dance industry is not just about making sure that the important decision-makers know you. WHAT they know about you is just as important as their knowing your name. One of the most important responsibilities of a professional (or pre-professional) dancer is to create their own reputation. Yes, it's important that directors and choreographers know you, but it's even more important that WHAT they know about you is positive. So key, in fact, that I've decided to spend an entire chapter on it.

You might ask what, exactly, is networking and why is it

important to a dancer? Good question. The simplest definition of networking is making relationships with people and keeping them. Sounds easy enough, right? It can be. So, why is the skill of networking particularly important to dancers? Ever heard the phrase "out of sight, out of mind"? That's why. Say you're a mom looking for a babysitter. Would you prefer to search online for "babysitters" or ask a friend or acquaintance for a recommendation? I would wager that 90% of babysitter-seekers would choose the latter. The same sentiment applies to hiring dancers. When a production holds an open audition for dancers, it's the equivalent of them searching the web for babysitters. You might find one babysitter (or dancer), but you never know what you're getting. The dancer that gets the job from an open audition could be talented but perpetually late or prone to injury or a pessimist or a poor team player. Rarely are negative attributes like this visible during the short audition process. That's why many of the folks "behind the table" prefer to hire the dancers they know. Or dancers that people they know. That's where networking comes in.

  Sometimes it works out that a producer or choreographer "rolls the dice," has an open audition, and takes a chance on hiring a cast of unknown dancers. This could be a great thing – one of those dancers could be you! Often, though, choreographers hire a mix of their "usual suspects" (dancers they know to be talented, versatile, and great to work with) and "newbies" (one or two dancers they don't know but are willing to take a chance on). Because dance is obviously a shorter career than most, producers and choreographers DO need to regularly add new young dancers to their roster to cycle in when their older folks go off to do other things. This factor is a young dancer's chance to get on "the list". More often than not, though, before offering an unknown dancer a contract, producers will ask around about you first. In this case, the more people who know your work and your personality, the better. And the better you are at networking, the greater the number of people that know you.

AGENT'S TAKE: Being new to the professional auditioning landscape means you will need to prove more than your skills. You will need to define your reliability, your commitment, and your professionalism. The industry talks; make sure the conversation they're having about you reflects

you in a positive light.

∽

It sounds like a lot of work for a producer or choreographer to check up on an unknown (or known) dancer, but often, it simply requires a quick text or phone call. When a director or choreographer hires a dancer, they are essentially committing to spending NUMEROUS hours with said individual. It's a pretty large decision based on very limited information, all things concerned. Choreographers, when they hire dancers, are often committing to spending eight-hour rehearsal days, numerous 8-12 or 14-hour shoot days (if it's an on-camera project) or numerous 7-12 show weeks (if it's a live event) with, well, pretty much virtual strangers. Whatever the project, the audition is inevitably the SHORTEST time that the dancer and the creative team spend together. Thus, it is in the people-behind-the-table's best interest to find out what they're getting into.

Let's say a choreographer likes you in audition, but they're unfamiliar with you and your work. Let's say he or she texts, say, the choreographer of your last gig or the director of the last dance company listed on your resume and they receive a poor review of your teamwork skills. Guess what? You're probably not hired. What if the producer calls folks from your last gig and they respond with a negative review of your work ethic. Guess what? Again, probably not hired. And what if the creative team happens to even just look you up on social media and the first thing that pops up is your drunken, partying, half-open-eyed Instagram feed? You guessed it. Not hired.

Most of the time, a dancer is either successful in procuring a job from the audition itself (and probable acquaintance-based background check) or someone on the production team knows and has already hired the dancer before the audition even takes place. These are the reasons networking in the dance industry is one of the most important and attainable "legs up" (pun intended) on the competition.

Regardless of specifics, the basics of human nature prevail. Humans, all other factors being equal, almost always choose the more familiar option over the less familiar. In fact, there is something called the Pareto principle that states that we choose the same 20% of our familiar options 80% of the time. That rule applies to producers, directors, and choreographers as well. Humans just gravitate toward what has been successful in the past and, more generally, what is familiar. That's just what we homo sapiens do. So, what is familiar? Well, there are many definitions of familiar.

Casting and directors/choreographers respond positively to many different variations of "familiar". The most traditional interpretation of this is that folks sometimes just plain hire their friends. In the dance industry, relationships with choreographers, directors, and casting directors are and will always be instrumental in the procurement of jobs. The long and the short of it is: the more friends you have, the more jobs your friends get you. ***Caveat: This only applies to dancers that have a baseline of technique and skill. Your friends aren't going to hire you if you're going to make them look bad on set. No relationship will replace hours of work in the studio.***

The other definition of "familiar" is the sneaking suspicion that a person has seen another person before. Whether a choreographer has seen your social media posts on their page, thinks they've seen you dancing with a music artist, or has a good memory of you in an audition setting, familiar is almost always GOOD. That's why just being out and about in the industry is a great thing to do. Take classes, go to shows, and participate in charity events. Once a person "behind the table" sees you a few times around town, you become a familiar face. And, again, familiar is good.

Agent's Take: One of the most essential elements is to get out of the house! Integrate into your community by going to see a spectacular show, by seeing a community event or a wonderful spectacular involving dance, singing and all elements within the entertainment industry. Surround yourself with individuals that are like-minded, well connected, and have the ability to speak to others that have the potential to further your career.

So, how does a dancer create and manage relationships with the decision-makers in the growing dance industry? Good question. Here are a few ways:
TALK

The first (and probably most obvious) step to successful networking in the dance industry is . . . talk to people. This may seem easy and obvious, but dancers, in particular, can struggle with being verbally expressive. Consider that the reason most dancers START dancing is because they prefer expressing themselves with their bodies over expressing themselves with their words. Even if a dancer is a naturally loquacious individual, they have inevitably still spent most of their free time being silent (aka dancing). As mentioned in the last chapter, I cannot express how important it is that dancers take some sort of public speaking or acting class if they find themselves without the gift of gab.

AGENT'S TAKE: Make sure to speak up. You may be a super nice person; however when you remain quiet it can be construed as defensive, conceited or negative. Make an effort to clarify your positive personality by being approachable.

Just talking to people can lead to innumerable potential future employment opportunities. Take for instance, me.

Three months after moving to Los Angeles from New York, a friend from the East Coast called to say that he was visiting Los Angeles and wanted to catch up. He also mentioned, "You HAVE to meet my choreographer friend. You guys will totally hit it off". Now, the evening he suggested to meet was at the end of a long, exhausting day and my preference of evening activities would have been sleeping. But, because of my fondness for my friend, I valiantly rallied and joined him and his "choreographer pal" for dinner. At dinner, I met his lovely friend who was currently working on choreographing her first Broadway show. He was right – we hit it off immediately, found out we all had numerous mutual friends and spent the evening telling stories and talking about upcoming projects. I was happy I had decided to join them.

As this choreographer was mostly working in New York and I had mostly retired from full-time dancing to move to the West coast, I didn't think about the possibility of future employment with this choreographer. I enjoyed the evening, joined her circle of friends on social media, and kept in touch out of the habit of networking that I had developed over the years. Also, I just kept in touch with her because I genuinely enjoyed her company and respected her work as a creator and educator. At that point in my life, I was not looking for any dancing jobs at all – I had just accepted a position teaching in the dance department at a college and was happy in my partial retirement from dancing.

Nevertheless, this wonderful woman who I'd had a personal and fun connection with, called me OVER ONE YEAR later and offered me a dancing job. Sight unseen. I had never auditioned for her in my life. (Though, I am assuming she did her due diligence and internet research on my performance skill set before making the call). This choreographer said she had just found a role/project that I was right for and was determined to convince me to take the job. So, I did take the job. And it was a blast.

That, in a nutshell, is the importance of networking, intentionally or unintentionally. Had I not taken the time to go out and meet, get to know, and keep in touch with this individual, I would have missed out on playing a fabulous role in a fabulous show at a huge theater in Los Angeles. (Incidentally, about nine months after that, I had the opportunity to hire one of my fellow cast members from THAT job to be part of the faculty at my school). And the circle of acquaintance and employment carries on . . .

AGENT'S TAKE: The circle of acquaintance and employment within the entertainment industry is ever evolving, therefore, making connections and staying connected can make a positive difference in future opportunities.

"Talking" rule number 1: Don't make the mistake of assuming which friends might be able to get you jobs.

I can say with full confidence that you NEVER know who is going to be behind the casting table. A casting intern can turn into a casting assistant in a year and a then suddenly they're a full-fledged casting director the next year. You also never know whom a choreographer, director, or producer is going to ask to assist them in the casting process. You might walk into an audition and recognize the person that stood next to you at the barre in ballet class the day before or the bartender at your local restaurant. Again, you never know.

AGENT'S TAKE: A good rule to remember is never to presume. It is not up to you to determine where you think someone else's career will end up, therefore be kind and keep a keen memory - - they may end up hiring you at some point.

The obvious advice is that you should treat everyone with the same gracious respect and genuine interest that any decent human being would. This seems to be a given, but you'd be surprised how many dancers do not adhere to this advice. I have seen dancers ignore or cast aside humans that they don't think are cool or influential enough for their time. And I have also seen this approach backfire royally. You can spot this type of dancer at parties having a conversation while not-so-subtly looking around for more important or influential people to talk to. Not only is that rude to the individual with whom they're having the conversation, but it is also terribly obvious.

AGENT'S TAKE: Everyone has value and deserves equal respect. Make an effort to give professional courtesy to everyone; make sure the courtesy is authentic and does not turn on and off. Being fake does not prevail.

For instance, I once worked on a particular Broadway show in which there was a young man who was tasked with overseeing the child performers (fondly known backstage at most Broadway shows as the "child wrangler"). Because most of the cast and crew didn't think he was "important," during the out-of-town tryout, most people completely ignored this young man; not inviting him to dinner, not including him in conversations, etc. I (and a close friend in the show) did not take this route. We took the time to get to know this young man, invited him to join us at social functions, and, well, treated him like ANY HUMAN SHOULD. It turns out, this young man's family owns a major franchise and about a year later, he asked my friend and me to perform at one of his family's (very large national) events. Where were the folks that were rude to this young man? Not performing on national television, that's for sure. The moral of the story? Just be a good human being. To everyone. And not because you think they can get you something. Because being a good human makes you feel great, it makes others feel great . . . sometimes you get to do fun things because of your kindness.

"Talking" rule number 2: The difference is in the details.

How do you make sure that you have the greatest probability of running into a friend or acquaintance "behind the table"? Again, TALK!!! Talk to everyone. Get to know the people in your community and be kind to them. Remember their names, what their interests are, and what they're working on. Details, in these instances, are everything. For every acquaintance, remember at least ONE thing about them that's interesting or unique and WRITE IT DOWN. For instance, if a fellow dancer happens to mention when you meet her that she's learning to make jewelry, remember this and write it down. The next time you see this dancer, greet her BY NAME, ask how she is, and mention her jewelry making. She will be flattered you remembered.

"Hi, Jane! How are you?" (Then really LISTEN to her answer and respond).

"Really? I will have to try that boot camp. You look great! You know what? I thought of you the other day when I passed this little jewelry boutique in Larchmont. How is the jewelry making coming? Is it fun?"

Chances are, Jane answers enthusiastically and you have a great conversation. Did you think of her in Larchmont? Maybe not. But you're thinking of her now, so . . . that counts in my book.

AGENT'S TAKE: Again, really LISTEN. Don't be that artist that is so wrapped up in your own world that you half-listen to others around you. You can learn much from others - listen.

Here's the point. Chances are, Jane Doe dancer remembers little to nothing about you after one brief meeting and feels flattered that you remember such a specific thing about her. After you GENUINELY mention this detail and GENUINELY care about her answer, she will then make a much more concerted effort to remember you in the future. And thus, a relationship is born. When Jane's director brother is looking for tall Caucasian hip-hop dancers who happen to tap dance on his music video-themed episode of CSI (and you fit this description), you'll hopefully be at the forefront of her mind, she will mention you to her brother, he will call you in for an audition, and you'll book an awesome gig.

"Talking" rule number 3: Don't be "that person."

The one specific thing you choose to remember about acquaintances to bring up later in conversation should preferably not be "business"-related. Or if it is, I would recommend that you choose something to chat with them about that you wouldn't be eligible to be cast in. Why, you might ask? The last thing you want Jane Doe thinking is that you care about her only as far as she can get you a job. Hopefully, you don't. Hopefully, you truly care about her and want to know her better. It should be a win/win situation. You make a new friend/acquaintance and you create a potential ally for the future. People are not pawns, and I highly recommend GENUINELY creating relationships that can last. You don't have to be besties with everyone and fill your social calendar with meaningless meetings, but you should remember people and give at least one crap about them because chances are, you'll run into them again. Trust me; it's a really small business.

Lastly, it should go without saying, but just be yourself. Particularly if a person is in a position where they could get you a job and you're aware of that, don't be weird. Don't find ways to spout your résumé or name drop. They know what you're doing. Just be normal. Please. People are people, no matter what. Trust me, a producer can smell weirdness a mile away and it does not smell like flowers. Just relax and try to be the truest version of your own fabulous self.

Agent's Take: Learn how to answer questions pertaining to the industry. For instance, know what aspects of your career you love most, what you have done, what you aspire to do, who the individuals are that you want to work with next, etc. These are important details that people will want to know about you; particularly so they can help you navigate the industry or even connect you to that perfect person that is looking for you in their next project.

LOG

Since you're probably busy filling your head with choreography and planning your very exciting future, you may not be able to remember all of these wonderful new acquaintances you're making in your industry. Never fear. That's why the spreadsheet was invented.

I highly recommend that you create a spreadsheet of acquaintances. I promise it will serve you AND your friends and acquaintances well in the future. Even if your spreadsheet is not perfect and you only update it every few weeks or months with very general information, trust me, after a year or so, you will look back on all of the people you've met and be glad you made notes.

Your contact spreadsheet should include the following information:

A) Name – First things first. Actually listen when people introduce themselves to you and remember their names. I, myself, am guilty of reading a person's facial expressions, body language, and other things while they're telling me their name. And then I immediately forget it. (I know that's not ideal and I'm working on that). If you have a habit of doing this, find a way to link their name to some physical attribute that you're busy noticing and make sure to repeat it to make sure you've gotten it right. If you don't happen to get a person's full name, that's fine! You'll get it eventually. Or not. Either way, make sure to log your new acquaintances in your spreadsheet. You'll be glad you logged the information you have.

I have numerous people that have started out on my spreadsheet as, say, "Stephen-from-David-Howard's-ballet-class-at-BDC" who have turned out to be either good friends, helpful acquaintances, or have shown up in future projects. If you happen to remember that Stephen-from-David-Howard's-ballet-class-at-BDC is into, say, performance art and the next time you see him, you bring up Marina Abramović's new exhibition piece at MOMA, Stephen What's-His-Name will probably become Stephen Nelson when you get to know him a little better. You and Stephen Nelson then become social media buddies, and the next time his friend calls looking for brunette aerialists, he thinks of you. How have you remembered the information about what Stephen What's-his-name is into? Well, you've logged it on your spreadsheet and before you venture out to David Howard's class at BDC, you simply sort your spreadsheet to show you your contacts that you've met in this class, refresh your memory on their information, and head out to make some new contacts. Easy as pie.

B) Contact information – The next thing you'll need for your industry contact spreadsheet is information on how to contact your new acquaintance. This can be an email address, social media name/handle, phone number, or any other way of contacting a person (maybe they work at a local coffee shop or teach a regular workout class). Sometimes it's not weird to ask for a person's contact information on the first meeting. Maybe you make plans to do a project together in the future. Or he/she needs volunteers for an instructional flash mob video for an industrial company in Berlin. Or she says she's willing to adopt your friend's cat and wants you to put them in contact with each other. Whatever. In these cases, an exchange of personal information is acceptable if not necessary. In some situations, though, blatantly asking for a person's contact information is TOTALLY WEIRD. This is where your good judgment comes into play.

If you do happen meet a new person, there are a few different levels of keeping in touch that should be heeded in order not to, well, be a total stalker. Instances like, "Jane, I can't wait to see the turquoise jewelry you'll make! What's your Instagram?" are completely acceptable. Situations like, "Hey, Starbucks Barista, you're a dancer, too? What's your cell number so we can keep in touch?" are completely weird.

(STRANGER DANGER: This should go without saying, but obviously, don't give a person you don't trust your contact information. Step away from the situation if an encounter with a person is ever creepy, antagonistic, or just plain sour. You will not click with every person you meet. That's fine. Don't force a connection.)

Here are some suggested levels of procuring contact information from a new acquaintance as defined by some general codes of social interaction:

1) You meet a new person, you know very little about them, but you share the same industry = "See ya later. Great to meet you". Don't weird people out by asking for their information if you don't know each other. Stalker-licious.

2) You and your new acquaintance made a personal or artistic connection, but were total strangers before your conversation

and chatted for less than 20 minutes = Instagram/Twitter

3) You have met a new person, acknowledged and confirmed that you have numerous mutual friends, and had an extended shared experience (i.e. a long wait at an audition or teaching at a weekend convention). And/or you two just plain hit it off as bosom buddies immediately = Facebook/Snapchat. It is a nice gesture, if you HAVE made a connection with a person, to hand them your own business card and say something like, "let's keep in touch". Chances are, they'll respond in kind and you have yourself a new contact.

4) You meet someone and you and your new acquaintance plan to do something in the future together that requires direct contact – i.e. he invites you to his upcoming show and offers you discounted tickets, or you find out you're neighbors, you have an incontinent Shih Tzu, and he has a dog walking business. = Exchange email addresses/cell phone numbers.

Obviously, these are not hard and fast rules, but they're pretty good guidelines, so keep them in mind when getting contact information from new folks you meet. The underlying theme is to abide by general social norms and err on the side of respecting people's privacy.

C) How you know/met them – This is a very helpful piece of information to keep in your contact spreadsheet. You may not, for instance, remember who "Tall guy Grant" is, but if your spreadsheet says "met at Sarah Carson's New Year's Eve party", you can mentally review the evening and remember who this person is. AND the next time you go a party at Sarah Carson's house, you can automatically sort your spreadsheet for "Sarah Carson's friends" before you head out for the evening. Then, you have a good idea of who will be at the party and what you've chatted about with them.

D) Physical attributes/specialties/skills – Not only is this a great category to have for further ways to remember people, but this is also a wonderful category in which to pay it forward. For instance, say you meet a male dancer that studies trapeze who happens to be 6'4" tall. You made his acquaintance on your last music video shoot and you know him to be a talented dancer, a good person, and a hard worker. Then imagine (and this happens all the time) you have a friend that mentions or posts on social media that they're looking for exceptionally tall male trapeze artists for an upcoming live performance with a well-known music artist. There you go! You can recommend your friend and pay it forward.

But, what if your tall trapeze swinger friend does not immediately come to mind? Guess what? You have your handy dandy spreadsheet in which you've entered your friends' special skill. You can quickly scroll down column D of your spreadsheet (or sort alphabetically by the column) and find any and all of your friends that have trapeze skills. Then, you recommend your tall high-flying friend to your other friend and DONE! You've done a good deed for both your friend that is looking for dancers and for the dancer himself. In addition to the general warm fuzzy feeling you get from people-connecting, both of these people now may feel that they owe you a favor.

Even if you don't know anyone that has that EXACT skill, you can recommend someone else that has a similar skill "just in case". This shows your pal that's looking for the talent that you care about their project and it shows your other pal with the similar skill that you care about THEM and respect them enough to recommend them. More on this topic in the "Pay it Forward" section, but this is one of the most important boxes on your spreadsheet.

E) Contact date and method – Many career coaches and agents posit that in order for a person to remember another person or product and connect them to future opportunities, they need to have come in contact with that person or product SEVEN times. This "Seven Points of Contact" theory is a great way to think of keeping in contact with directors, casting folks, and choreographers. More on this in the next section, but you definitely need to include on your spreadsheet WHEN you've been in contact with each of your acquaintances and HOW you've been in contact. This keeps you from being a nuisance ("Come see my midnight show!" "Read my pointless blog!") and it also keeps you from staying quiet for so long that your hard-earned acquaintances don't completely forget you.

UPDATE

It is imperative that after you meet a person, specifically a choreographer, director, producer, casting director, or any folks actively involved in choosing participants in projects that you're interested in, that you KEEP IN TOUCH!!! Time is finite, but unless you're keeping track of it, it can bend enormously with perception. Take, for instance, your audition for a well-known music artist's last tour. You felt great in the audition. The choreographer was staring at you the whole time, you felt confident about selling the choreography, and you made it through the first three cuts. Six months later, Such-and-such choreographer is holding another audition for a different project and you think, "He must remember me – it wasn't that long ago that I auditioned for him." Meanwhile, Such-and-such choreographer has done a minimum of fifteen new projects in the past six months and has no idea who you are. This is the exact reason that, if you're interested in working with a specific person or on a specific project, you need to make sure you remain in the forefront of their minds.

How do you do that? Well, let's start with the commonly accepted and previously stated idea that people remember other people and products after they have received SEVEN POINTS OF CONTACT from said person or product. These points of contact can come in various different forms. A choreographer can see you at an audition and then on a well-shared social media post and then at a dance class and then at a party and then in an email, and then on a commercial and then at a benefit concert. And THEN they KNOW and remember who you are. Done. Seven encounters, both electronic and in person. So, updating key players in the industry is a key element to your continued employment. (It doesn't hurt to keep your friends up to date as well – remember, you NEVER KNOW who will be "behind the table").

Here's when you should get in touch with your contacts and let them know what's up with you:

• **You've just met them and enjoyed your interaction with them.** The most important time to contact a person is directly after your first interaction with them. If it's a fellow dancer, a well-timed "I think you're great, I loved chatting with you, and let me know when I can come out and support your stand up comedy career" is a perfect interaction. (You've contacted them, so they feel worthy of your time, you've remembered something about them that's outside the dance industry, and you've offered up support on one of their projects – triple whammy). Also, the sooner you contact them after you meet them, the more likely they will be to remember you.

It's also appropriate to contact a choreographer or director via peripheral social media if you have a good experience with them in an audition. They're human, so it makes them feel good, too! "I just had the most positive and inspiring audition with

@kickitchoreographer for his next show! He was just as awesome in person as I had imagined!" on your Twitter feed is a win/win situation. First of all, @kickitchoreographer may see you (and your beautiful dancing Twitter profile photo) on their feed. Second, your social media pals see that you're actively working to get a job and are positive about it (and positivity about an audition makes folks assume that you did a great job). Double whammy. Everyone enjoys positive feedback on social media; from the hottest choreographers to your favorite flight attendant.

• **You've done or are doing something cool and you think it's good enough for people to see.** There is no better way to remind people of your work than humbly updating them on an upcoming project. For instance, "Hey, Such-And-Such. Just wanted to let you know that if you want to see me shake my stuff as a dancing bunny, I'll be appearing on tomorrow's episode of Modern Family on ABC at 9 pm! Somehow, I always guessed that my television debut would be as an animal. I hope you'll check it out and consider me for any future projects you have coming up!"

You can update your contacts about a piece you've choreographed, a music video in which you're dancing, a charity concert performance you have organized, a new open class you're teaching at a local studio, an inner city dance class for which you're volunteering, or dancing with Lady Gaga at the Grammys. The point of the contact is that you let everyone know that you're working on some project in the industry. The more a dancer works, be it self-generated or not, the more experienced they're perceived to be (and the more new contacts they're bound to create). Everyone wants to hire an experienced, philanthropic, in-demand dancer.

• **You get new representation.** There are few things that are more awkward than a producer calling an agent or manager that you have parted ways with to offer you a job. It's just . . . awkward. Please let people know as soon as you sign on the dotted line that you've changed or added representation. Also, updating choreographers, directors, and producers that you've got new reps shows that somebody wants you (hopefully in addition to them). If you've signed with a reputable agent or manager recently, it's pretty solid proof to the world that you're marketable and that a professional has validated that by making a commitment to spend their time and on furthering your career. There's power in numbers.

The more people want you . . . the more people want you. If you're updating your peers on new representation, a tasteful general post to social media will suffice. Assume that a few of your contacts might be slightly covetous of your good fortune.

• **It's been a while.** This is a tough "update" category. See, you don't want to go more than six months without reminding folks that you're available to dance and that you're an awesome dancer and person. But, reminding a person of, well, nothing is both a waste of their time and a little desperate-looking on your part. First things first, if you haven't done something in six months that is worth telling people about, you should have. These days, there is no excuse for dancers to not generate their own projects. Don't wait for someone to hire you. Make your own work! MAKE IT WERK! (Okay, you knew I had to do it). Shoot a dance-based web series, shoot a music video on your smartphone, organize a live in-studio performance for a charity with your friends, create your own website, mentor a young underprivileged dancer. WHATEVER! Keep doing things! Even if your update is "I've decided to take up fire baton twirling – here's a picture of me in class", that's awesome! People want to know that you are taking charge of continuing your own personal growth and technical and artistic development.

While these are general guidelines of when to get in touch with your gaggle of fellow artists, they're the only times to do so. Get creative and connect. I spent a few months where I took a different person to lunch every Wednesday. Do that for a year, and you've got yourself 52 new allies in the industry.

The flip side of keeping people in the loop about how awesome a person and dancer you are is to NOT OVER-SHARE. The last thing you want to be is annoying or, well, someone's spam, but the prime directive is to consistently be in the forefront of the minds of as many of your contacts as possible. There is a very fine line between "I-remember-her-she-was-great-in-that-music-video-audition" and "Oh-my-God-I-wish-she-would-stop-clogging-my-inbox-with-updates-about-her-clarinet-lessons". This is why it's imperative to keep track of when you've directly contacted people with updates about your doings. This is specifically important when contacting and keeping in touch with choreographers, directors, producers, casting directors, and other folks that don't have a lot of time. (Though, let's be honest, none of us do).

Agent's Take: Most importantly, don't forget to be the most authentic version of yourself. Be genuine – people see though those who are phony. No one is like YOU; no one has your dance ability, your look, or personality. Therefore, there is no other person better to be than yourself. Network your authentic self!

PAY IT FORWARD

One of the best ways to take advantage of your new contact list is to turn your new organization skills into a benefit for everyone else! The more you converse with people in the industry, the more you realize that everyone wants or needs something. Choreographers are looking for a producer. Producers are looking for directors. Directors are looking for talent. Agents are looking for new clients. Dancers are looking for new agents. Teachers are looking for students. Students are looking for teachers. The list goes on.

I guarantee that if you spend time talking to any person in the industry, you will learn that there is something specific that they need or want. It could be a hip hop teacher looking for extra work in a dance studio or a choreographer looking for a dancer that can tap dance in roller skates. OR it could be un-industry-related. Perhaps you speak to a producer that's looking for a unique handmade gift for his wife. Guess what? You now know a dancer that custom makes jewelry. This is a great opportunity to make an introduction, and in this scenario, everybody wins . . . particularly YOU! Say you are successful in referring your jewelry-making friend to your producer friend. Your jewelry-making friend is super grateful for the new client, and your producer friend is thankful that he does not need to contribute any more brain space to figuring out an appropriate gift. Again, everyone wins.

Your jewelry-making dancer friend will now definitely remember you and may or may not feel like she owes you a favor. Same thing goes with your producer friend. In essence, you have solved both of your acquaintances' problems, so you win twice! And it's more than likely that you've made the world a better place while doing so.

This is only one example. There are countless ways that you can become a problem-solver in the industry. You should consider yourself to be first and foremost a "people connector". Someone needs a recommendation for a tap teacher in Sydney, Australia? You're their guy/gal. Check your spreadsheet. You might know someone that has worked in Australia. Someone needs a recommendation for an upscale vegan restaurant in downtown Los Angeles? Check your spreadsheet. You probably know the owner of one. And if you don't, you probably know someone that's vegan. Text your favorite vegan and ask for recommendations. Your vegan pal will be happy to give business to her favorite restaurant and potentially her favorite restaurant's proprietor and your other friend will be thankful for the recommendation. You get one more point of contact with two more people and everyone wins.

Networking is one of the most overlooked and undervalued skills in the dance industry. It's also one of the easiest tools to employ. Meeting people, making acquaintances and friends, and keeping in touch is much simpler than doing a standing back tuck or a quadruple pirouette while holding a squirming live kitten. Take advantage of the friendships you make, enjoy the company of other people, keep track of folks, and pay it forward. Chances are, it will provide you more opportunities than you could ever imagine. And if it doesn't? Worst case scenario, your networking prowess makes you new friends, gets your friends jobs, and helps your new friends make new friends of their own.

AGENT'S TAKE: Some of the most important aspects of one's career are developing tremendous networking skills. There are a number of incredible tips that can help you better market yourself and feel more comfortable. Networking is not easy, especially since dancers are used to working with their bodies. It is essential when working with an inner voice to learn to speak literally through your speaking voice as well.

Learning how to communicate with others is just as important as training within different genres of dance. Once you have the basic tools as a dancer (understanding the movement and your authentic you), it is important to communicate with your community of dancers to help network and build your platform of what you want to become within your given profession.

Remember, you must be able to clearly state who you are,

what you do, and your career goals to effectively give the listener a firm grasp of who you are. This may sound impossible at first, but once you are able to pinpoint exactly what you do, and where you want to take your profession, you will be clear on stating where you see your career heading. Know your intention.

     Sometimes we feel like we are wasting time going to events again and again and we feel disappointed that we have not received immediate gratification in our career. Improving your career is not like shopping for a new wardrobe. You cannot simply purchase a career that fits you immediately. You have to keep shopping yourself around and asking for direction from others to see if they are connected or potentially have a job tailored to you. Remember that when you connect with those that create job opportunities they may not have something immediate to offer, however, they may have or know of a project in development for which you would be a perfect fit.

4

Branding

One of the questions I'm asked most often from dancers in every discipline is "What is my brand?" It seems that every dancer wants to know how they're seen from the outside and how this pertains to their place in the industry. From folks looking to get jobs on Broadway to dancers that want to book the new Celine show in Vegas, EVERYONE wants to know how to find their corner of the dance market. "Brand me! Brand me!", Is the overriding chorus I hear every time I do a lecture on the dance industry. And rightly so. It's a very important thing to know.

However . . . I have news for everyone. While I (or any other reputable professional in the industry) can give an outside perspective of my overall impression of you and how I think you would fit into the dance industry, ultimately, you are the only person that has all of the knowledge necessary to decide where you fit in. YOU are the only person that can decide what your "brand" is, how to market yourself, what jobs to audition for, and how to cultivate your "look." Of course, you should ask professionals in your chosen industry and take into account their advice on how they view you, but nobody, super famous casting director or other, can ultimately tell you what to do. It's kind of like asking a stranger what you want for dinner. How do they know? Do they know about your peanut allergy? They can say you look like you would enjoy sushi, but without all of the information you have, it's pretty pointless.

The best "brand" is your own individuality. It's the ballerina with alopecia, the Barbie B-girl, or the contemporary dancer with one arm (not kidding – search Youtube – I recently watched a gorgeous pas de deux featuring a woman with one arm and a man with one leg, and I'm sure they work ALL the time). The best way to find your ideal brand is to capitalize on the things that make you different. Figure out the things you do best and then focus these toward the corner of the dance market that will appreciate your uniqueness in the most welcoming way. Most importantly, (and sometimes most maddeningly for some dancers), the key is to **just** do "you." And you should work very hard do "you" as authentically and enthusiastically as possible.

AGENT'S TAKE: You and your brand will evolve over time. The objective is to resonate with who you genuinely are and the goals you are seeking within your career. The industry is ever-expanding; therefore the amount of opportunities to promote your brand is constantly growing. Having a clear vision of who you are will provide a clear image to those who are interested in representing, hiring, and working with you. Your brand is a reflection of you -- - make sure you are realistic and authentic with the reflection you allow the industry to see.

Here are a few key points you can use to make sure that you know what you're putting out there . . . and to making sure that it works (or . . . WERKS).

FIND YOUR PERSON

One of the most effective exercises I've done to help define and refine my brand is one of creating my fictional ideal client. The key here is the word fictional. If you say, decide that all you want to do is dance for Mia Michaels every day, you risk mentally being open to other potentially wonderful options. So . . . take a bit of time, even a few weeks, and come up with your ideal client - the person in the industry that will be most likely to choose you first for all of their projects. Usually, this is a choreographer. But, it can be an audience member, a producer, a director, or a casting director. Decide who (fictionally) would want you most and then decide WHY.

For instance, when I first did the "find your client" exercise (a LOOOONG time ago), I decided that my ideal client was the Broadway producer that needed an ensemble member to dance well enough to be considered a "dancer" in the ensemble who could cover the high soprano notes and sing and act well enough to understudy a lead or two. Oh, and I decided the more specific niche was more traditionally scored and themed shows and revivals (as opposed to more contemporary rock shows). That may sound very specific, but the more specific you are with your ideal client, the more specifically you can develop your brand. (While I REALLY wished I were cool enough to be belting high notes and wearing fishnets and fingerless gloves in Rock of Ages . . . well, I wasn't. And I'm glad I was honest with myself about that.)

One good, honest look in the mirror showed what I had to work with. I will always have a kind-looking wholesome-looking face and a solid base of classical vocal and dance training. I could have worked very hard to learn to riff and belt E's, dyed my hair black, gotten numerous piercings, learned to break dance, and dropped the F-bomb on all of my social media. That might have changed things a bit. But, WHY? All of that effort would be so much more taxing than just being me. And I probably would not have been as successful. The people "behind the table" can smell a poser from a mile away. (Do people even use the term "poser" anymore?) There is a place in the dance industry for every type of dancer. Even for those "types" that have not yet been invented, there is more than enough room for you to create your own niche. Again, I am vehemently opposed to people trying to be a "type" that is unnatural to them. That's energy that is much more appropriately directed toward making the "you" that you've got even better.

So, back to the "find your client" exercise, once I had created a specific picture of my ideal client, I thought long and hard about what they would want to see in an audition. The first question was: If I were to go to an ensemble audition for a new Broadway show, would I go to the dancer audition or the singer audition. (Most Broadway shows have separate ensemble auditions for singers and dancers. Both groups end up singing, dancing, and acting, but the dancers usually dance first and then sing after they make a cut – and vice versa for singers). When I assessed my strengths, I figured that the dance combination would be significantly harder than the singers' post-cut dancing combination, so I figured if I could make it through the dancer combination cut and then sing really well, it would impress my ideal client much more than if I did the opposite. So, I did that.

I also chose a song from which I knew most dancers would shy away. "Glitter and Be Gay" from the musical Candide is one of the more difficult songs in the musical theatre canon to pull off (it took a LOT of work to make this song fabulous), but when my ideal client producer put my coloratura notes against my cohorts' selections from Chicago and Gypsy, I definitely stood out. I also did the unthinkable (at the time – now it's a bit more mainstream). I changed clothes after I danced. I wanted my client to see me as a viable candidate to understudy a lead on Broadway, so why would I walk into the room in a sweaty leotard instead of a nice dress and heels? I wouldn't. Everyone else at the audition looked at me like I was a bit crazy, but more often than not, I was called back or offered the job.

Now this is one example of playing to your ideal client, but this approach can work for every part of the dance industry. Say, you decide that your ideal client is a choreographer that looks for raw, grounded dancers that are genuine performers and super great at contact improvisation. Great! Now you can do your research and brand yourself and audition accordingly. How? Use common sense. If this is the client you have chosen (and you've done your research and found a choreographer that fits this description), chances are, you don't wear leopard print to his/her audition. You also probably wear minimal makeup and don't inappropriately paste on a cheesy fake grin while you're dancing his/her choreography. You get the idea.

AGENT'S TAKE: A wonderful ability an artist can acquire is what I call the "Chameleon Effect." Having different techniques and a wide range of abilities will allow you to make quick decisions and seamlessly apply those skills to a project. Defining a specific characterization for your role on a project will allow you to apply your Chameleon Effect while still allowing you to maintain your individual brand and remaining within the boundary of a productions vision. Pushing yourself as an artist to try new areas that are uncomfortable will not only expand your range but will clarify what areas you are most drawn to. To grow the most, you will need to try opportunities that are out of your safe zone.

MAKE IT MATCH

The second step to solidifying and perpetuating your brand in the wild world of dance is to make every part of your persona match. This includes your headshot, website, Instagram, dance photos, Snapchat, YouTube channel, wardrobe, and resume. There are many decisions to be made across all of these platforms. What is your particular dancer's take on life? Are you eternally positive and cheery, are you sarcastic and edgy, or are you deep and introspective? There is no wrong answer as long as you're genuinely yourself. The tone you decide on should match your brand and all of your social media and promotional materials should fall in line. What's the color scheme of your website or blog? What's your chosen font? Are you calligraphy, hot pink, and yellow? Or are you more chalkboard, black, and orange?

I know, I know. "Does this all REALLY matter? Shouldn't I just be a good dancer and get the job because of that?" Yes. You should. And sometimes you might. But, hopefully, you're building a CAREER, not just a string of individually acquired jobs. And the basis of a long-lasting career requires that you first build a solid brand. Do you have a catch phrase or a specific dance step that sets you apart? Use it to your advantage and make it part of your brand. This includes making this dance step or catch phrase part of your website, social media, and even wardrobe. For instance, I can't use the word "sass" in a sentence without thinking of Rachelle Rak (her catch phrase is "Sas attack" – spelled with one "s"). Has anyone been on Cat Cogliandro's social media? "Work Your Quirk" is on the top of almost all of her posts and she even sells tee shirts sporting the phrase. My last example is a brilliant dancer and choreographer named Ambrose Respicio who has a signature dance move that is the hybrid of a layout and a "cooter slam." He calls it "Shablam" which pairs very well with his first name – Ambrose – get it? Shablam-brose? And he has performed this step pretty much everywhere – including in front of Lady Gaga at the Grammys. All three of these people have incorporated these phrases and ideas throughout their work. This attention to detail is memorable. And memorable + talent = jobs.

Are these brands, themes, phrases, and steps the things that make these artists successful? No. Are they things that help folks remember how successful and brilliant these artists are? Yes. Remember the lesson from the networking chapter that the more a casting director or choreographer sees your name or work, the more likely they are to call you in to an audition? Well, yes. If you have developed a specific and memorable brand, it makes them all the more likely to remember you and thus, call you in for an audition.

The other thing that needs to match your brand is . . . you

guessed it . . . your look. While a "look" is much more an important part of the commercial dance industry than concert dance or Broadway, it is still important. We all want to live in the perfect world where talent is the sole basis of adjudication in an audition setting, but we just don't. Yes, your choreographer may be looking out for technique and great storytelling ability, but your producer may not know anything about either of those things. Your producer may just want to hire people that he or she thinks are "hot" or "edgy" or "cool" (or the opposite – yes, there are those jobs). For better or for worse, the producer (with or without a lot of imagination) always gets a pretty hefty say on who is hired for their projects.

Fortunately, it takes minimal effort to go to a class or an audition looking the part. Note: your personal version of the part. If you are lucky enough to be asked to an invited call dance audition, it was probably either from someone on the creative team viewing your headshot, reel, social media, or website. Or you got the invitation after your agent called casting and encouraged them to look at one of the aforementioned things. Hopefully, your "digital package" is already curated to represent your brand and this is why they called you in. If your brand is the funky-geeky-nasty hip hop dancer, your digital package reflects that, and you are asked to audition for a project because of that, PLEASE show up looking like that person! The folks behind the table get pretty grumpy when the funky-geeky-nasty dancer they were excited to see shows up as a very different type. (Incidentally, if you have a few different "looks," it's always good to check on casting sites or ask your agent which photo was submitted so you can do your best to replicate that specific look for the audition).

A good way to test out different looks is to dress for class the way you'd dress for an audition. While it is significantly less important that you look fabulous for a class, you can test out different things to wear while dancing. For instance, you may think a particular set of overall shorts are perfect for an audition, but when you wear them to class, you realize that you can't battement higher than ninety degrees. It's better to make this discovery in class than in an audition, trust me!

Essentially, you should think of yourself and all of your materials, including your look, as a matching set of stationary. While the envelopes, writing paper, and note cards in a box of stationary are different objects, they have the same look and feel and match up beautifully when put together. Are you ecru parchment and calligraphy or magenta card stock flipping your recipient the bird? The possibilities are endless, but most importantly, they have to be authentically yours.

AGENT'S TAKE: It is incredibly important that your brand is a true reflection of you. Make sure your ability, your image, your attitude, and your intent are in alignment. Having those details in line make for a positive trajectory in your career path - be a shooting star!

SPREAD THE WORD

There is absolutely no point in having a fully developed brand if you don't spread the word. "If a tree falls in the forest . . ." and stuff. These days, dancers have the vast opportunities afforded them by the growing arena of social media at their fingertips. If you don't know how to use social media, you've either been under a rock for the past ten years, or you're from Mars. Either way, it's ok! Even if you're a cave dweller or a Martian, social media is pretty darn easy to use. Just waddle your little extraterrestrial bootie over to a computer and a website called YouTube and they have tons of tutorials on how to use, well, anything. If you're a human and a functioning native resident of Earth, then get to it. Social media is a working dancer's best friend.

How do you spread the word? Good question.

• Find a trend and ride the wave. By the time this book is published, these will no longer be a thing, but anybody remember the #mannequinchallenge or the #alsbucketchallenge? If you do any of these well, people searching for these will watch your version and like it and you have a new fan. Heck, while you're at it, why not create your own hashtag? If you happen to even find ten people in the world that like your work, you have ten more fans than the average Joe (if you and Joe's moms are both #11, they automatically cancel each other out). If, like, Cat, you #workyourquirk consistently and do it well, other folks will start to follow suit. And then perhaps you start trending. And then you get more followers. More followers = more visibility = more opportunities.

- Post photos when you're working on set or rehearsing something cool (Note: ALWAYS ask your production first in case it's a project that does not want publicity before it airs – many a dancer has been fired for leaking information about, say, a live television event too soon). On the other hand, many projects (often the more indie-based ones) love it when they get a little boost in online visibility. So, just always ask. In an age where many of the top social media outlets are photo- or video-based apps, dancers can garner a lot of attention and fans with good quality, well-curated content, and cross-pollination with the fan bases of the project or other individuals involved.
- Find people with similar interests and engage them. It's an easy search if you happen to be an elven-looking nature-loving ballet dancer to type "ballet" and "nature" into a search engine and then add or engage with folks that enjoy the juxtaposition of these two things. Conversation breeds connection, and chances are, you will find a few new followers and maybe even make a new friend or two. Hiking in pointe shoes, anyone?
- GET OUT. Go to dance events, classes, and parties (but please don't get wasted – that completely undoes all of your efforts). Remember when you're socializing that you're perpetuating your brand, so represent! If your brand is a hippie, free-spirited contemporary dancer, don't show up to a major event not looking like your brand. Particularly if you happen to know that press will be at your event! Make sure to make the "you" that you're presenting in your red carpet "step and repeat" photos matches the "you" that you're selling in the audition room. Then, when your new paparazzi post photos of you with your new friends at this event to websites like Wireimage and Getty Images, and then later when potential employers do a web search for your name, they get a good idea of what you're selling. Which is . . . let's say it again – the best version of the most authentic you.
- Post videos of your work. Do you know how many people get job or audition opportunities just from their social media accounts? No audition required? Tons. If you're one of the large numbers of people in a developed nation on the planet Earth, you probably have a smart phone. Use it to your advantage. Show everyone your best moves. And more importantly, show them in an interesting way. A beautifully executed aerial is much more

interesting on a mountain at sunset in a floaty dress than in sweats in an artificially lit dance studio. The more artistic you are with your dance AND your cinematography, the more folks will want to watch.

AGENT'S TAKE: Social media has been one of the most significant areas for an artist to promote their brand. There has never been a better time than the present for an artist to self-promote. Due to social media, the visibility of an artist can be changed in the blink of an eye by providing millions of individuals the ability to see you as the artist you are. Make sure what you are posting is a true reflection of you. Every post you make will define your talents, your viewpoint, and your tone. What you say in posts can be easily misconstrued and misinterpreted, so be clear in your message and be true to your brand. As social media continues to evolve, make sure to stay current and savvy to new areas and platforms that can expand the visibility of your work and your brand.

Nowadays, with the accessibility of practically any individual via email, cell phone, and social media, dancers can spread their brand recognition literally around the globe. (Incidentally, it might be worth your while to look into gigs and trends in dance in different countries - if you haven't traveled extensively, do your research online. If you limit yourself to thinking only nationally, you may lose some super cool international job possibilities!) It takes some dancers years to find the most effective way to market themselves in the dance industry, so if you're not completely clear, don't fret. The most important thing to remember is to represent your truest self and put in the legwork (pun intended). Diligent creation of content with a professional and well-timed release, be it photos, video, or text, does not come easily. You put in the work and the thoughtfulness, and you will hopefully reap the rewards and recognition. But, if you put your time and energy in promoting a product that is not marketable or genuine, it's a waste of time. When it comes to branding, in the wise words of my favorite New York-based drag queen, "You do you, boo. You do you."

5

Representation

To get an agent or not to get an agent. A question even Shakespeare asked . . . to an extent, anyway. I would like to officially go on the record as saying: get a freaking agent. If you have auditioned for representation and you have not yet been successful, that's totally fine. Keep working consistently and it will hopefully pan out. Eventually, though, if you're working the business of the business correctly (and you're a more-than-moderately-talented dancer), I believe representation will seek YOU out. No matter whoever chooses whom, chicken or the egg, please do acquire representation when you can. Future You will thank present You, I promise.

Unfortunately, in the dance industry, there are peripheral companies and seemingly exciting employment opportunities that are just plain hoaxes. The only surefire way to know what's legit and what's not-so-legit is to have a professional (agent or manager) look out for you. It's more than worth the ten percent of your eventual pay to not end up shooting a "music video" in some random "up-and-coming" rap star's friend's basement in your underwear so that you can get a free lunch and the video can get a whopping 943 views on YouTube. By the way, ten percent of zero dollars is still zero dollars. The ten percent pay chunk off of the pay from the jobs you get through your agent is the price you pay for the opportunity, connections, and guaranteed protection. Protection of your time, protection of the limited usage of your image, protection of your right to breaks/meals/safe working conditions/wardrobe limitations, and many, many other things. Oh, and by the way, if that paycheck from your last gig doesn't happen to appear in your mailbox within 90 days, you don't have to be the person calling the producer or choreographer to ask where the heck your money is. Your agent is. And, for the record, most agents make really great "bad guys" in many situations.

Let me tell you a cautionary tale about a young lady named Denise:

Once upon a time, our hypothetical friend Denise attended an audition she heard about on social media and booked a music video job. (Great job, Denise!) Let's follow Denise as she learns a few good life lessons on her first dance gig.

Denise is so excited about her new job dancing on her first music video and receives an email telling her the shoot date, location, and time to show up for said shoot. A few days later, Denise excitedly arrives at a warehouse in downtown Los Angeles with makeup, a few wardrobe options, and a few pairs of shoes she can dance in. She is welcomed by the second assistant director and immediately asked to sign a five-page contract. Denise is told that she must sign the contract before she can proceed to hair and makeup, but as she peruses the pages, she reads the words, "Dancer relinquishes all rights to dancer's image, partial or complete, both video and still images, in perpetuity over all media outlets." This sentence has a lot of commas and general words and, even amidst all of the new job excitement, gives Denise pause. Well, guess what, folks? IT SHOULD.

Despite her initial reservations, Denise signs the contract, not wanting to be late to set, and heads to wardrobe where she is issued a mesh bra, a thong, some fishnets, and a pair of platform shoes that are two sizes too big. This gives our friend Denise even further pause. First, she has already been told that she will be doing multiple fairly complicated dance steps while performing on a very small raised platform, so she begins to worry that she might twist an ankle in the shoes that were very obviously not intended for ANY of the movements she plans to perform. Also, there had been no mention of any kind of provocative wardrobe or nudity in the audition or audition notice, and Denise happens to have a very conservative family and a very protective husband that works in local government. The thought runs through her head that had she been told what she would be wearing; she probably would have turned down the job. She decides to take matters into her own hands.

Denise intelligently approaches the wardrobe folks, expresses her concern and asks for another wardrobe option . . . but all of the other options are significantly more revealing or reserved for other dancers. What should she do now? Denise is already on set and has signed a contract. Not to mention, the choreographer of this music video is someone she has been cultivating a relationship with for some time. She assumes the choreographer will write her off if she walks off set on the day of shooting, so she decides to go against her better judgment and head to set in her transparent underwear. Denise valiantly manages to not sprain her ankle or fall off her platform while shooting the video and feels that she has solidified her relationship with the choreographer as one of his new reliable and talented dancers. She hopes he will begin to call her for future projects and continues to keep in touch with him about her endeavors.

Then, a few months later, she realizes that she has not received her $50 check for the 12-hour music video shoot. She decides to call and ask where it is, but . . . who should she call? When she looks back at her copy of her contract, there is no contact information listed for the producers of the video. The only person whose information she does have is her new most-promising contact for future employment, the choreographer. The last thing she wants to do is upset her first legitimate contact in the business. So, she waits.

Finally, six months after the project has wrapped, she decides to suck it up and make the call (after all, she thinks, she compromised her values and relinquished the use of her image until Earth no longer exists to these folks, so the least they can do is give her fifty bucks). Her new favorite choreographer grudgingly agrees to look into it. Small win. Soon after that, Denise's brilliant thong-clad locking has garnered a plethora of hits and positive comments on social media. People know her – she's on the way to a great career in dance! Denise is stoked . . . even though she is wearing no clothes, her family is mortified, and STILL has not been paid. Then, the same footage of her dancing appears on a new platform on the web - an ad for the music artist's new brand of sneakers. Why is this bad, you might ask?

Well, Denise just painted herself into a corner. She signed a document on set that allows the producers of this project to use the footage of her dancing in the video. For anything. Anywhere. Forever. Including promoting an unknown brand of sneakers. FOREVER. In the commercial world, this is considered a brand conflict. So, say, if five or ten or even one year down the line, a mainstream sneaker brand has an audition for a national network commercial, Denise can't go. She has a shoe conflict. That potential

$30,000 commercial has been precluded by the fact that she signed a $50 contract she didn't read or understand. Oh, and she still hasn't been paid that $50.

Now, folks, this is a VAST exaggeration of what can happen in the dance industry, but it can and does happen. Dancers enter a confusing and complicated industry at a very young age and are asked to function at an extremely sophisticated level. In most industries, one is not expected to conduct him or herself in a manner that is discerning and savvy until they've been in their chosen profession for a number of years. Many people do not run their own business until at least the age of 30 or 40. Dancers run the business of themselves as soon as they sign up for their first audition. Are all young dancers savvy enough to read and understand a ten-page contract that is full of legalese while under the pressure of producers in a time crunch? Maybe. Never underestimate the intelligence of a dancer. BUT it's hard to know what you don't know in these situations. Particularly if you're fairly new to "the business." So, in short, there are a lot of dancers that could use some help. Including myself.

A good agent would have protected our hypothetical friend Denise from the hard life lessons she learned in her music video shoot. Her agent would have read the contract ahead of time and would have been able to either have the producer rewrite it or advise her not to do the project. An agent would have also been able to get her paycheck! The most impressive thing I've found that a good agent does is read between the lines. Agents know exactly what to look for in a contract because contracts are a large part of what they do for a living. If you have the opportunity, my advice is to let the professionals do what they do best. We've all heard it, but when it comes to contract negotiations, its way better to be safe than sorry.

AGENT'S TAKE: An artist's representation is their first line of opportunity and defense. As an agent, I have defined myself (alongside those that have dedicated their professional careers as agents) to being an advocate for the betterment of artists' conditions, compensation, credit and creative potential.

By definition, a talent agent (or booking agent), is a person who secures jobs for actors, authors, film directors,

musicians, models, film producers, professional athletes, writers, screenwriters, broadcast journalists, and other people in various entertainment or broadcast businesses. In addition, an agent defends, supports, and promotes the interests of their clients. Talent agencies specialize in supporting the interests of their clients, either by creating departments within the agency or developing entire agencies that primarily or wholly represent one specialty. For example, there are modeling agencies, commercial talent agencies, literary agencies, voice-over agencies, broadcast journalist agencies, sports agencies, music agencies and many more.

WAYS AN AGENT CAN MAKE YOUR LIFE SIGNIFICANTLY EASIER

- **Agents read the fine print**

Agents know what to look for in a contract. It's one of the hugest parts of their job, so let them do what they do best. If you're about to go on tour, do you know if you'll be required to book your own travel from city to city? Will you be paid extra to do an aerial silks piece as part of the show's finale? Are you required to go to all of the rehearsals for new dancers even if it means you don't have a day off? Can the recording artist that you're touring with require you to go to parties on your off-time? Can the touring company video a performance and sell DVDs of it without giving you a cut? Will your per diem change when you go to countries where the exchange rate is more than double that of your dollar? Will you be fired if you dye your hair a lighter color? ARE THESE QUESTIONS YOU KNOW TO ASK?? They're questions an agent asks and answers every day.

Despite the legal jargon, you should also know when a contract leaves something OUT of the fine print as well as when to look for key phrases IN the print. For instance, if you're teaching for a dance convention on the weekends, wouldn't you want a clause in your contract that they can't book you on flights that leave before, say, 6 am? Or if you live in Newark, wouldn't you want a clause stating that these folks can't book you on a flight that leaves from, say, Laguardia before 6 am? Wouldn't that make your life oh-so-much easier? (And save you precious cab fare?) Yes, I think it would.

- **Agents can be the "bad cop."**

Ask any agent, and they will tell you that it's perfectly acceptable to blame a surprising lot of things on them. "I'm sorry. My agent told me not to sign anything until she looks at it. Can I send her a quick pic of this addendum?" That is perfectly acceptable. And it's the right thing to do. (There's usually a good reason a producer brings you a last-minute addendum after you've already signed a contract . . . and it sometimes includes things that are not in your best interest.)

Agents are also great at calling casting directors to check and see what the heck is up. Say you have an offer for a smaller-scale project, but you had a recent kick-ass callback for a much larger-scale project. The problem is that the smaller-scale project starts in a few days and would potentially overlap the larger-scale project. (Champagne problems, right?) This is a great job for your agent! They can call and at least get a gauge if you're still "in the mix" for the larger project. AND when your agent calls a casting director to let them know you have multiple offers, they can make you sound super talented and in-demand. (On the other hand, if you personally make that call, it can sound a little desperate or naggy. Some folks without representation ask their friends to call on their behalf as their "personal assistant" or "manager." Incidentally, this is not something that I would recommend unless the friend you choose is exceptionally well spoken and knowledgeable about, well, almost everything.)

Finally, in the "bad cop" category, agents can subtly chase down your paychecks. You know, that random benefit concert you performed in three months ago and haven't received your $200 check? Yep. They'll make the call. (In a perfect world, agents wouldn't ever have to call producers and hound them for checks, but it does happen from time to time.) And the last thing most dancers want to do is ring a producer they met only once to demand their dough.

- **Agents are your biggest cheerleader**

Guess what? The more money you make, the more money your agent makes. Is there a more incentivizing situation in the world? It baffles me that dancers complain that their agents aren't working for them. Of COURSE they are! If you were an agent, wouldn't you work hard to show off the talented individuals you personally chose in order to make more bank for both of you? I sure would. Agents want you to succeed, and it's their job to make sure they give you every opportunity to do so.

One of the harsh realities of the dance industry is that there are some auditions for which only an agent can get you in the door. Some gigs will only audition dancers that have representation because they have a limited number of time and/or space for their auditions. On top of that, not every dancer with representation will always be invited to audition for all of the jobs for which they want to audition. It's a fact of life. Everyone, including all of those famous dancers you know out there, has experienced at least a few times where their pals were called in for an audition and they weren't. It happens to the best of us (though it happens to the worst of us significantly more often). If the casting director or choreographer chooses to ask you to attend an audition that is an invited call, great! Go and kill it. If, though, you are not initially invited to one of these auditions, your agent (aka personal cheerleader) can call the casting director or choreographer and attempt to talk them into changing their minds (and inviting you to audition).

When an agent calls or emails casting to procure an audition for their client, industry folks refer to this as "pitching." Agents pitch their clients on a daily basis. (And if your agent isn't pitching their clients, it may be time to find one that does). One of the most common questions dancers ask of potential agents is, "How often do you pitch?", meaning, how often do you fight to get a few more of your clients seen for a project. It's also good to know HOW an agent pitches. Do they simply send an email that could get lost in the shuffle or do they pick up the phone and call a specific casting director until they answer? Incidentally, THIS is the type of agent that you want to be your cheerleader to take you to the super bowl. (Maybe literally – halftime show with Rihanna, anyone?)

Incidentally, do you know what agents will use to "pitch" you? They'll use your reel, resume, photos, or (last resort usually) social media. These should all be current and good representatives of you and your brand . . . before your agent sends them to casting directors (see chapter 4). Imagine if you were a casting director, you only had space for one more dancer in an audition room, and two different agents pitched two different dancers as candidates for that last spot. Would you choose the dancer that you could not see dancing anywhere or would you choose the dancer with the flattering, slick, and professional media package? Preparation = good work ethic = great future employee. No brainer, right?

- **Agents know people**

One agency can have hundreds of clients in different parts of various industries. The same agency can represent writers, dancers, hosts, actors, producers, musicians, choreographers, and sports personalities . . . all in the same building. While the group of agents at an agency generally split up their roster of people based on discipline, they still often work in the same area and share ideas. A great agent can help you make connections with people in the industry that you may not have been able to meet without them. When an agent is successful in pairing more than one of their clients on a project together (for instance, booking a dancer they represent on a project that's choreographed by one of their clients), it's a payday double whammy for them (and it's great karma). Not to mention that they've hopefully set up a partnership with that dancer and choreographer that will carry on to future projects.

Has anybody wondered how so many seemingly random pairings of music artists come about? Do you honestly think that Eminem and Elton John met randomly at a rager and decided to collaborate on "Stan"? I don't actually know, but I'm guessing . . . probably not. Generally, these introductions are orchestrated by representation, either to diversify an artist's audience or to bring a lesser-known artist into the mainstream world. The same thing happens in the dance world as many agents that represent working dancers also represent choreographers and directors as well. Many a dance agent has sent many a group of dancers they represent to workshop the choreography of one of their up-and-coming influential choreographers.

For instance, this happened to me with my "theatrical agent" (that's LA-speak for my agent that represents me for projects on film and television). My wise agent booked me to do a table read of a new feature film that was being funded by a huge production studio . . . just because I happened to be one of his clients that listed speaking French my resume. I arrived at this reading and found a large room of recognizable working actors and producers. As it turned out, my agent represented the writer of the film and virtually all of the remainder of the cast as well. It was a pretty awesome experience. (There is rarely an official audition for this type of thing – a table read or working on pre-production for projects are mostly "who you know" situations.) You never know what will come of this kind of project. Sometimes, if you do a great job in the reading or choreography work session, it can lead to you being cast in the actual project. Worst-case scenario, though, if you don't get cast, you still probably did a great job and made a room full of new influential contacts. That's a pretty good worst-case situation.

AGENT'S TAKE: Having representation provides an artist the vast experience, connections, and resources that a well-established agency has. Having an agent is not required, but does help facilitate the artist getting jobs (concerts tours, script access, auditions, brand endorsements, etc.). In most cases, casting directors, or other businesses solely seek talent agencies to find the artists for whom they are looking. An agent is paid a percentage of the artist's earnings (typically 10% for union projects and up to 20% for non-union projects). Various regulations govern different types of agents. These regulations are established by artist's unions and the legal jurisdiction in which the agent operates. There are also professional associations of talent agencies.

For example, in California, because most talent agencies work with lucrative contracts, the agencies must be licensed under special sections of the California Labor Code. The California Labor Code defines an agent as a "person or corporation who engages in the occupation of procuring, offering, promising, or attempting to procure employment for artist or artists." Managers are not licensed or held to the special sections within the California Labor Code.

However, agency representation goes far beyond submitting an artist, organizing the audition details', negotiating a booking, reviewing and securing the contractual agreement, invoicing and making sure payment arrives in a timely fashion. An agent will also work closely in making sure the artist's materials are current and effective for submitting purposes, as

well as meet and stay connected on the goals of their client. Additionally, representation consistently maintains their industry connections and has early knowledge of upcoming projects.

HOW TO GET AN AGENT

By now, you're probably thinking, "Wow, those agent folks sound pretty darn great. Where can I get one?" That's a really good question. Realistically, it can be very difficult to find and procure a dance agent, particularly in cities that have a large market for dancers, (i.e. New York, Tokyo, Los Angeles, etc.). Even some of the most talented dancers I know struggle to find and keep representation in today's crazy-competitive industry. Don't let that deter you, though. The persistent bird gets the worm. Here are the most popular ways to garner dance representation (in order of their effectiveness).

They Find You

The MOST effective way to find an agent is not to find them at all. They find you. It's the perfectly movie-worthy scenario. Say you're minding your own business taking class at The Edge or performing at a benefit for CTFD when suddenly a dapper and important-looking person swoops past all of the other dancers in the lobby and approaches . . . you.

"I really love your work. Are you currently represented by anyone?" he says briskly.

"Um . . . no. Not really." you reply. (You think about surreptitiously mentioning your uncle Joe who called a producer and pretended to be your manager to get you $50 more on a recent web series. But you wisely decide not to).

"Give my office a call. We'd love to have you come in."

Then this super-important and enviously busy-looking person breezes out of the room leaving you in a cloud of Armani cologne and holding an embossed business card.

Sounds just like a movie, right? Well, it does happen. Not very often, but it does. It happened to me, actually, after a performance at City Center in New York. I'm a unicorn. Okay, not really, but agents are really always on the lookout for new talent. They don't just check out the people that send them information.

Agents want to find the next undiscovered talented superstar, right? (Remember, the more dough you make, the more dough they make.) So, the more you're out and about, the more likely it is that an agent will see and recognize your talents. Now, granted, if you suck at dancing, this will never happen to you. Sorry. Find another passion.

If you are, in fact, a unicorn, and someone does approach you, please do your research. It may be a legitimate and awesome agent, but it also may be a scam. Some folks out there pretend to be "agents" and then ask actors and dancers to pay them; either a monthly fee, pay to take their class, etc. As flattering as the attention may be, please don't fall for these scams. A legitimate agent will NEVER ask you to pay them up front. Always research an unfamiliar agency's website, look over their client list, and/or call a union you belong to before you physically go to a location to meet a stranger. Stranger danger, people. Stranger danger.

You are referred to them

The second-most effective way to nab representation is that someone that the agency knows and respects refers you to them. Your referral can come from a fellow dancer, a choreographer, or even a manager (see the manager section at the end of this chapter for more information on alternative representation). The more highly the agent regards the person who referred you, the more likely they will be to check out your stuff, come to a show you're performing in, or invite you in for a meeting. This is a great foot in the door!

Before all of this, though, again, you must do your research. Research the dance agents in your area, their clients, and what kind of projects they work on. You can do this research on the web, but it's also always great to ask around. The dance industry, even the global dance industry, can be a very small place and all agencies are different. Some agencies are more rooted in the world of musical theater dance, and some agencies are more adept in booking their clients on national commercials. That's not to say that an agency that is known for its commercial department would not be able to book you in a show in Vegas, but you just might be dealing with a smaller corner of the agency. Either way, do the research before you ask anyone to refer you to any agent so they don't refer you to an agent that may not be the right fit for your skill set.

Once you've found the top three agencies that you think might fit you (YOUR top three picks, not the top three in the

WORLD – big difference), ask your contacts in the industry to make an introduction. But choose your ambassadors wisely. Here are indicators that a person would be a good agent-ambassador:

- **They have known you for a good amount of time**. Don't go around asking people you just met to introduce you to their agent. That can sound pretty desperate. And if they refer you and they don't know you, they risk tarnishing their own reputation with their agent. You want a referral to an agency to be an enthusiastic recommendation, not an obligatory passion-less email.

- **They know and respect your work.** Don't ask a person that has never seen you dance to refer you to an agent. Think of it as recommending a restaurant that you have never visited to a friend for his or her tenth wedding anniversary. Would you do that? Hopefully not. Most wise dancers and choreographers will not make a blind recommendation either. If you haven't done enough good work to have people that know it, GET IN CLASS! And get on the stage. And in front of the camera. No excuses! Additionally, it's not enough for a person to know how you dance. You want to ask a person to refer you to an agent that knows your personality, your work ethic, and your commitment. The adage is true. A salesman sells more when he believes in the product.

- **You are not their competition**. It's best, unless you have no other option, to ask a person to refer you to their agent that is NOT your direct competition. Think of it from your friend's point of view. Such-and-such agency has twelve tall Asian tap dancers, and the person you want to refer you to their agent is one of these twelve. If you happen to be a tall Asian tap dancer as well, why would your friend want to make herself one of thirteen contenders for prospective auditions instead of one of twelve? She probably wouldn't. Choose someone else.

- **They LIKE their agency.** Seriously, there are a lot of people in the world that say they don't like their agent. In fact, there are people that will say that they HATE their agency. There are two reasons people say they don't like their agent. First, it might not be a good agency. So, you don't want to be represented by this agency in the first place. Bullet dodged. Second, the agency is, in fact, a reputable agency, but your friend that says they don't like the agency is either not getting a lot of auditions from this agent, OR they have a negative relationship with this agent. Either way, don't ask for a referral from a person that doesn't like their agent. Think about it: If you were an agent and you didn't have a good relationship (either not strong or negative) with one of your clients, would you go out of your way to see a dancer that they recommended? NO! So, don't waste your time. Choose an advocate that has a good relationship with their representation.

Relationships are key in the dance industry and the more you make (and the stronger they are), the more opportunities they allow. A referral to an agency is a huge step in the right direction.

You go to their open call

Many dance agencies have open auditions periodically throughout the year to seek out new talent. You can find these auditions on an agency's website, on their social media, or through your network of friends in the industry. If you are a trained dancer in the style that the agency is seeking, it never hurts to show up to an open audition. I always think of open calls as free dance classes . . . classes that have the potential of turning into future opportunities.

Remember when you go to open agency auditions that you should bring an updated headshot and resume, you should dress to represent the best version of yourself, and that you should PERFORM! Tell a story with your dancing rather than just showing off your virtuosic technique. Inevitably, the dancer that can act while dancing is significantly more likely to be noticed (and hopefully signed).

You blind-contact them

A "blind contact" is the act of contacting an agent (or other industry professional) before they have any idea who you are. (Thus, the "blind" part.) Whether it's an email or a tweet or a hand-written postcard, if the recipient does not personally know its sender, (no matter how beautiful or talented you are), you can be their equivalent of office junk mail. Ever how ineffective a blind contact is, dancers and actors still insist on giving this method of contacting agents the old college try. And while it is often all for naught, I will maintain that a 0.05% chance of catching an agent's attention is better than a 0% chance. (And it's 100% chance that I made those numbers up.)

I will go on record as saying that the blind contact method works very rarely . . . but I will also go on record as saying that you also never know. Many agents will say that sending a letter, email, postcard, or private message is a waste of a dancer's time and money. But there are others that acknowledge that now and again; the stars align and this blind contact method works out in their (and the dancer's) favor. The blind contact method of seeking representation works best for dancers with a very specific look, skill, or physical quality.

For instance, if a well-known music artist is looking for bald heavily-tattooed women for his/her new tour, and you happen to send a postcard on the exact day when an intern is scouring their client roster for dancers that meet that specific description, chances are, you are going to get a second glance from this agent's intern. That is, if you, in fact, are a bald heavily-tattooed woman. (The same thing goes for casting offices as well as agencies – if you happen to be in the right place at the right time, you may get yourself an audition.)

Otherwise, though, blindly contacting an agent is not your best chance at nabbing representation. Your chances of receiving a call or email from an agent as the result of even a well-thought-out letter or small gift will still, unfortunately, fall on deaf ears (or . . . blind eyes). In fact, most mail or electronic communication of this sort probably never even reaches your intended recipient. It simply goes into a file marked "extensively-tattooed bald dancing women" that is organized by an intern for future reference (and often forgotten about).

Now, there are some very sneaky ways to get your (hopefully fiercely photographed) mug in front of the most influential people in a traditionally structured agency. This was a secret that was passed down to me from a very successful Broadway and now television star, so don't tell anyone . . . I mean, anyone else. IF you send your information in a small envelope that is hand addressed (basically, an envelope that looks like it holds a check rather than an 8 x 10 headshot and resume), you can slightly increase the likelihood that your mail will at least be opened and partially read. Why? No smart agent is throwing anything in the trash that could even possibly be money. If you do this, though, know that you have about 2-3 seconds to grab their attention before it goes into the recycle pile. So, use your one sheet of paper and your first words (or photo) wisely!

AGENT'S TAKE: Agents desire to develop an open line of communication with the artists' goals, build connections, and

provide opportunities to expand the artists' career. The artist is a reflection of the agency they are signed to, therefore, when an agency signs a client, the agents are agreeing to proactively work on the artist's behalf to initiate connections prior to being compensated for such efforts. Additionally, the better the commitment and connection between the artist and agency, the more positive the results. Loyalty goes a long way, especially when an agency is instrumental in developing an artist's career. Within the dance community, most agents are active supporters that attend events, contribute to union committees, and promote artists' rights within the industry. Agents are the direct liaison between the artist and production, a confidant, and a provider of guidance for the artist. These responsibilities go above and beyond the average business workweek and facilitate a consistent connection between the artist and opportunity.

Obtaining and maintaining a professional rapport with an agency can make a profound difference in an artists' career. Having experienced and reputable representation that can handle all business negotiations, review all contractual agreements, and elevate opportunities is essential for an artist. This is particularly important in an ever-changing environment that incorporates multiple entertainment mediums (film, television, digital content, branding, live stage and commercial).

The long and the short of it is that representation can be one of your most influential assets in the dance industry. Because of this, though, dance agents are in high demand, and it can be very difficult to find an agent to ask you to sign with them. If you don't have an agent, please be patient and remember that most people don't. Agents are constantly bombarded with dancers fighting for their attention, and if you don't happen to be the person that catches it at first, it's by far not the end of the world. One of my favorite sayings is, "Keep consistently doing good work and eventually someone will notice."

This business of dance is all about who you know . . . and most of the time, the person at the top of the list of influential people is your agent.

MANAGERS

A manager is a very different type of representation from an agent. An agent is required to abide by the rules and regulations that are set forth by performers' unions (i.e. SAG/AFTRA, Actors Equity Association, AGVA, etc.), they contractually take ten percent of a dancer's wages off the top (before taxes), and they generally are less involved in the minutia of your career than managers (there are some exceptions). Managers, on the other hand, are not required to abide by any union's rules and regulations, generally take 15% of a dancer's gross income, and are (or should be) more heavily involved in the details your career than agents.

Many dancers, at the beginning of their careers, often have a choice between an agent and a manager. Neither choice is wrong. I think the best analogy that compares agents and managers is to imagine them as choreographers and stage moms in the competitive dance world (the choreographer is the agent and the manager is the stage mom). An agent, like a choreographer, provides a dancer with the steps and opportunity to succeed; they choose to hire you in an audition, tell you what to do on stage, and then go their separate way and let you do your thing. I liken managers to stage moms (the cool ones, not the crazy ones . . . usually). Managers can do the same thing as agents, but they're more actively involved in helping dancers figure out the smaller details of their careers. A manager will, for instance, help you navigate and (sometimes) run your social media or set up events and parties for you to attend that may lead to future relationships. If you're the type of dancer that has many facets to your career (i.e. dancing, choreography, book writer, producer, blogger, social media personality, etc.), a manager might be the right choice to help seamlessly meld all of those aspects into one cohesive brand/career/you.

Some agents are great and some managers are great. The choice is completely up to you when you're choosing representation to pick one or the other (or both!). Though, if you're a dancer that is going on auditions and working on getting a performing job (rather than juggling numerous brands/careers/companies), an agent AND a manager may be overkill. Remember, if you're a great dancer, everyone will want a cut of your dough, but you don't have to choose to sign a piece of paper that says you should give it to them. If you think your representation, agent or manager, is not working for you, advising you, getting you auditions, or making connections for you, they're not holding up their end of the bargain, and you should consider concluding the relationship. (Many contracts have a clause that if your representation does not get you an audition within a certain number of months of signing, your contract can be nullified). If you have an agent and a manager and think that you could have the same awesome career with just one of your two sources of representation, you should consider choosing one.

Managers, because they don't have to abide by union rules, do have some freedoms that can be beneficial to a dancer. Some managers agree to take only five or ten percent of a dancer's income if they also have an agent (which effectually saves a dancer from shelling out a whopping 25% of their wages BEFORE taxes – 10% to their agent and 15% to their manager). Some managers make deals with their clients to only take a percentage of their pay if it's a job that is a product of an audition that their manager specifically set up themselves (not one that the dancer found on their own). Some managers take care of the social media of their clients or take responsibility for the upkeep of websites and correspondence. Mangers can be great! But remember that all of that greatness comes at a price. Just be sure that you're willing to pay for it before you sign on the dotted line.

One of the things that can get dicey about managers is also one of the things that can make them great: they are not specifically required to adhere to a predetermined set of rules. Thus, if you are considering signing with a manager, do your due diligence and check in with numerous sources as to the reputation, effectiveness, and tenacity of the management company with whom you want to sign. There are innumerable horror stories in the dance industry about dancers that have had huge disputes with their managers due to either lack of transparency on the manager's part or just downright shadiness. In short, when it comes to managers, err on the side of caution and sign at your own risk . . . or reward!

6

Unions

When most people think of unions, they usually imagine a group of coal workers out in some remote small town in America huddled together with cardboard signs picketing for higher wages and better work conditions. (Or is that just me?). If you're like me, you entered the world of dance not caring one little bit if you joined a union or not. Unions seemed to me like a far-off thing that I would never need. I just wanted to dance, not to band together with fellow dancers to (as I imagined) tick off the folks that would potentially hire me by fighting for higher pay and things like health insurance. (Obviously, this was the very naïve and erroneous outlook of an inexperienced young person - myself). When I jumped (feet first) into the industry, I literally would have PAID someone (instead of GETTING paid) to be in a dance company. (And I did – I practically worked for free for the first two years of my career).

When you've been around the block a time or two, you will realize that unions are pretty important to dancers, whether you are in one or not. Not unlike other groups of people that create and uphold legislation, unions that deal with the dance industry are sometimes a dancer's double-edged sword. (By the way, if you happen to be able to swallow one of those, it's a super-marketable special skill.) In other words, joining a union can help protect you on the job or, on the other hand, being part of a union can sometimes keep you from getting jobs. A smart dancer knows which unions to join and when to get in, get out, and (sometimes) get around these often confusing groups of performers.

First of all, let's define what a union is. While I'm quite happy entertaining my previous image of lines of muscle-bound coal workers, a union consists of much more than that and they actively help employ and protect millions of people in hundreds of different vocations. A union is any group of people that organize themselves in order to have a say in how their workplace(s) are operated. When workers unionize, they can influence how they're paid, conditions in the workplace, job safety, benefits distribution, and other things that have to do with their specific occupations. Basically, folks get together and, for instance, say, "Hey, Joe Schmo Production Company, we are overworked, so we refuse to rehearse until you agree to give us a ten-minute break every three hours." Now, that's a very generic example, but you get the drift.

The good thing is that most of the formation of unions has already been taken care of by our dancer forefathers (and foremothers). There are numerous unions that govern dancing work, and there are an infinite number of benefits and pitfalls to joining (or not joining) them. We will discuss each one of the unions that effect dancers one by one in this chapter. I urge you, if you are even remotely inclined to skip to chapter 7, please be as disciplined as you are with your pliés and don't. Educating yourself on even the rudimentary details about unions affiliated with dance is one of the most proactive things you can do for your career. If you're any kind of successful in the industry, you will have extensive interactions with many unions, and you'll thank yourself for learning about them ahead of time.

AGENTS TAKE: The standards that have been initiated by the unions for the betterment of artists' conditions are to be celebrated. It takes many dedicated individuals to set such provisions in place, in addition to time, research and continued commitment. It is the responsibility of every artist to understand why unions have been established, and how their standards can be improved. As the industry evolves, union standards will need to be reviewed, revised, and will have to detail new standards within the emerging areas in the entertainment field.

If you want to see change in standards, get involved and be a part of the needed effort by voicing your opinion. There is always room for improvement of standards, and getting involved is an essential manner for an artist to understand how rules were set and how you can be a part of making them better.

Here is a list of the most prevalent unions that are affiliated with the dance industry and a little bit about each of them.

Actor's Equity Association

About AEA: The Actor's Equity Association, or "Equity" for short, oversees performers and stage managers in most Broadway and regional theater musical theater productions and national tours. It was founded in 1913, has over 50,000 members and is a member of the AFL-CIO (stands for American Federation of Labor and Congress of Industrial Organizations), which is a kind of union for unions.

Why to join:

If you want to be in a Broadway show, you must join the Actor's Equity Association. All Broadway shows work under the Actor's Equity Association, so even if you're not in the union before you get a Broadway job, you'll have to join to start working at your new job.

All Broadway shows and national tours are required to have a minimum of two auditions every year that are open to any current Equity members (most people call the union "Equity" for short). Which means that even if you don't have an agent or manager, you have the opportunity to wow casting directors for all Broadway shows and union national tours twice per year.

Regional theater jobs also are required to have Equity principal and chorus auditions as well (if they're a "union house" – meaning they're a theater that is contracted to hire union performers). Again, you're guaranteed to be at least seen by someone from the creative team.

Actor's Equity Association has specific minimum salary levels for different contracts that producers are required to uphold.

AEA has a very extensive list of rules and regulations that apply to auditions, rehearsals, and shows. For instance, according to AEA, if you're in rehearsal for a new Broadway show, you're required to be given breaks after specific periods of time. And they're not kidding about how specific your break is. Here's a word-for-word cut from a production contract (that, incidentally, is 171 pages in length and covers, like, everything): "In addition, there shall be a break of five minutes after each 55 minutes of rehearsal or 10 minutes after each 80 minutes of rehearsal for each Actor. All Actors rehearsing aerial stunts shall be on the ground and unclipped prior to the commencement of their breaks."

How to join:

There are three different ways to join the Actor's Equity

Association.

Somebody gives you an awesome job. The first (and most dramatic) way to gain admission to Equity is to be offered a job that requires that you join the union. This is a veritably rare scenario and is pretty hard to obtain. I had personally witnessed this scenario only once when a friend of mine and I went to an open chorus call audition for one of the Broadway revivals of Gypsy. We were numbers 352 and 353, and he booked the Tulsa understudy within the week. My very talented (and perhaps slightly lucky) friend was catapulted from the $400/week non-union job that we both were working at the time to a $1381/week Broadway chorus contract (in 2003). And he's never looked back since. Again, this is an extremely rare occurrence, but when it happens, it's simply magical. I guess he's a unicorn as well.

The second way you can join the Actor's Equity Association is to join through a "sister union" – basically almost any other union other than AEA. You can join AEA if you're already a part of one of the following unions:

SAG-AFTRA – Screen Actor's Guild – American Federation of Television and Radio Artists

AGMA – American Guild of Musical Artists

AGVA – American Guild of Variety Artists

GIAA – Guild of Italian-American Actors

If you've done the work to obtain membership in one of these reputable unions, the Actor's Equity Association is all, "Your family is my family" and you're in. Keep in mind that the fabulous gathering of individuals that is AEA and protects and oversees thousands of actors isn't cheap. Even if you join the party via a friend of a friend (i.e. a sister union), the cost of joining the Broadway union party is now over four figures (before the decimal), and you're required to cough up at least $400 of it and a written statement from your parent union (saying that you're actually working and in good standing) when you apply.

The third way to join the Actor's Equity Association is the most laborious, but definitely the most fun. Dancers can join the union by becoming an "EMC," or an Equity Membership Candidate. The EMC program allows candidates to use reputable theatrical work to count towards eventual Equity membership. For instance, if you're working in the ensemble at a theater that employs union performers, (but you're non-union), dancers can earn points toward their union membership. When you earn 50 points, you're in! The time-consuming part is that one week of work in a union theater equals one point. So, basically, 50 weeks of (generally) fairly low-paid work dancing in regional theatres around the world equals an express pass to the AEA club. Most regional musical theater jobs range from 4-7 weeks, so dancers generally have to book anywhere from 7-12 individual gigs (and work them all) in order to gain membership access. That's a pretty time-consuming prospective endeavor when, statistically, a dancer stands to book less than 20 percent of the Broadway, touring, and regional gigs for which they audition (WAY less). In short, that's just a lot of auditions.

That seems like a lot of time, but sometimes, before a dancer hits their 50 weeks of employment in an AEA house (theater), they have the opportunity to negotiate union membership as part of their contract. For instance, if a dancer has worked for Awesomesauce Regional Theatre for more than two shows and the producer folks know them and respect them, Awesomesauce Regional Theatre can negotiate with the union to "buy the dancer in" to the union. Meaning, a producer can give a dancer a "fast pass" (The Amazing Race, anyone?) to union membership. (This can be a pricey endeavor for regional theatres that may not have a lot of excess dough, so if this doesn't happen to you, it doesn't mean that your bosses don't like you!) It works the same way as the first scenario with the Broadway contract. Basically, you get a first class ticket to Actor's Equity Central and the producer is paying for it!

*** There's one loophole to the EMC candidate membership situation (face it, there are loopholes to EVERY situation). If you join another sister union (i.e. SAG or AGMA) AFTER registering for the EMC program, you can choose to join Equity after 25 weeks instead of 50.

Responsibilities of membership:

First of all, just be a good freaking human. The performing world is small and everyone knows everyone. Particularly in the Actor's Equity Association. Make the union a better place, will ya?

Actors are charged an (at the time of this publication) $100 registration fee (that will be credited against any future Initiation Fees) to join the EMC candidate program. In addition to that, there is a $1,100 initiation fee that must be paid within a maximum two-year period after joining.

Basic annual dues is currently $118 per year and is billed twice per year ($59).

If you're one of the lucky dancers that is offered and works a union job, you owe AEA 2.25% of your gross earnings (don't worry – they take it out of your paycheck before you get it!)

Benefits of membership:

Actor's Equity Association sets forth minimum salaries for all of their contracts (every type of contract has a different minimum amount). They also have pre-negotiated (for every type of contract) extra pay for additional duties, overtime rates, hazard pay, rehearsal breaks, days off, the maximum number of shows, dressing room standards, and many, many other things a dancer might not think of (until things go south).

AEA has already negotiated health benefits, pension, and 401(k) benefits for their members for each type of contract. (Dancers receive health insurance through the Equity-League Pension, Health and 401(k) Trust Funds and qualify for six months of coverage after working 11 weeks or 12 months of coverage if they work 19 or more weeks in a calendar year).

The union guarantees payment to actors if your producer is less than on the up and up and decides not to cough up the paycheck (they're bonded).

Equity provides supplemental workers' comp insurance if you're injured while on the job (over and above the state-provided monies).

They regulate how agencies relate to and deal with clients and keep an eye on agent/dancer contracts.

You get to go to all of the AEA members-only auditions. For a list of all Equity auditions in your area, go to www.actorsequity.org/castingcall

Finally, AEA has TONS of member discounts including free tax assistance through the Volunteer Income Tax Association, access to The Actor's Fund, Career Transitions for Dancers (CTFD), the Actor's Federal Credit Union, and a plethora of seminars, career counseling, and general helping out with any performing business-related stuff.

A personal note: I cannot begin to list the number of times that I have been so thankful that Actor's Equity Association has set up such specific rules for their dancers. The producers and stage managers I have worked with over the years have followed the rules and regulations set up by the Actor's Equity Association as sacred law, and I'm even more thankful for it in hindsight. When our choreographer rehearsed a dance piece well into a break time and was forced by stage management stop, I was thankful for the opportunity to finally get some water. When I performed potentially very dangerous aerial stunts eight times per week, I was thankful that they required our stagehands to check my rigging before every show. When I was unemployed and couldn't afford to pay to have my (very complicated) taxes prepared, VITA (Volunteer Income Tax Assistance) did them for me . . . for free. And even when I didn't know or care what a 401(k) was, AEA did. And they had my back. I'm proud to still call AEA part of my posse.

AGENT'S TAKE: Support your industry by being an active participant and educating yourself on the unions. If you are already a member of a union and not clear on what they stand for, make sure to do your due diligence to be informed. Yes, there may be areas that you may not agree with. If that is the case, become involved and voice your opinions in those areas. Attend union meetings. The more you know about what has been established and what it took to get such standards in place, the more that knowledge will help you craft solutions in new areas that need to be addressed. Get involved and educate yourself. Some artists will complain about areas that need improvement within a union. Instead of complaining, be the positive voice to help implement an effective and smooth resolution.

SAG-AFTRA

About SAG-AFTRA: SAG/AFTRA is the merged new super union of the original Screen Actors Guild and the American Federation of Television and Radio Artists, both of which were founded in the 1930's. SAG-AFTRA oversees the work of actors, dancers, singers, stunt people, voiceover folks, hosts, recording artists, journalists, and many other entertainment professionals. Including dancers. And there are now around 160,000 members of the union around the world. If you're working on a film, television show, commercial, web series, or music video, you'll more than likely be working under a SAG-AFTRA contract.

Why to join:

Pretty much all of the higher-profile and more lucrative on-camera projects are SAG-AFTRA projects. And, once you attain a level of experience in front of a camera, you'll probably have to join the union in order to keep working. What happens is, if you're a non-union performer and you're hired on a union gig, your producer must submit something called a Taft-Hartley report to the union (the name Taft-Hartley refers to the Labor Management Relations Act of 1947 that restricts the activities and power of labor unions). If you do this in one of the 25 right to work states (like Georgia, Texas, or Virginia), you have to join the union after a certain number of these Taft-Hartleys.

If you're a dancer that works regularly, you will want to take advantage of the copious super mega benefits that SAG-AFTRA has to offer – see the benefits section below.

Being a member of SAG-AFTRA carries a good amount of clout in the industry. If you're a member of the union, a reputable producer has hired you on a reputable project, you've paid the union's hefty initiation fee, and you've eliminated for yourself the option of less high-profile non-union work (unless you sneak and do non-union work on the DL which I highly discourage in today's social media-frenzied industry). All of this tells producers, directors, and choreographers that you are serious about your career and you're willing and ready to play with the big dogs. This also clues them in to the fact that you have done enough work to warrant membership.

How to join:

You can join SAG-AFTRA if you're already a member of an affiliated performer's union. Performers that have been paid-up working members of AEA, AGMA, AGVA, or ACTRA for at least one year can join SAG-AFTRA (you have to have worked, though – at least once as a principal dancer in the union you're using to join up). You can make an appointment at your nearest SAG-AFTRA office to set up an admissions appointment to figure it all out – make sure to bring a paycheck stub or paperwork from the payroll company of the union you want to use as your gateway union with you.

SAG-AFTRA membership is offered to dancers (and actors and other folks) who work one gig as a principal or three gigs as a background dancer (actor). These gigs must be covered under the SAG-AFTRA collective bargaining agreement, and you must submit paperwork to prove your employment.

Responsibilities of membership:

SAG-AFTRA has the heftiest initiation fee of all of the unions. New members must pay a one-time-only fee of $3,000 alongside the first semiannual dues when they join. Ouch, right? Here's a good thing, though. SAG-AFTRA now has an initiation fee loan that is offered by its member-owned credit union – AFTRA-SAG Federal Credit Union. You can make up to 24 monthly payments with discounted interest rates with some monthly payments of just over $100 per month. Or you can just put it all on your credit card like I did and pay for it for the next ten years (#whatnottodo). Ah, the crazy choices of youth.

SAG-AFTRA charges a much more palatable annual base dues of $206. You can save this amount in car rental and theater ticket discounts alone.

If you're a working guy or gal, SAG-AFTRA also collects 1.575 percent of your earnings under union contracts up to $500,000. If you're earning more than that, hire an accountant and they'll take care of it. **Note: If you join the union right after working on a SAG-AFTRA project where you were Taft-Hartley-ed, you may have to pay this 1.575 percentage on what you already earned.

Again, one of the responsibilities of being in such a great union is being a good human. It's an honor. You also should take the time to learn a little about how your union works – who are the main folks that make the decisions, what are your benefits and rights as a member, and what are the different contracts that are offered by the union. All of this good information can be found on their website: www.sagaftra.org and I recommend spending a fun evening with a glass of wine learning about your new future group of coworkers, allies, and supporters.

Benefits of membership:

SAG-AFTRA takes great care of their members by negotiating daily and weekly wages for all types of contracts, making sure working conditions are safe and sanitary, overseeing residual payments, and even helping casting and producing folks find performers' representation.

SAG-AFTRA also has an extremely developed pension, health, and retirement service for its members. When you work under a contract with producers that have signed the Collective Bargaining Agreements with the union (and they've paid up), if you're a union member, you earn credits that go toward pension and health plans. Both SAG and AFTRA have a minimum dollar amount and/or minimum amount of working days that members must satisfy in order to be eligible for future benefits. (So, you can't just have benefits without working for them – duh).

You get to learn stuff! SAG-AFTRA offers its members classes, workshops, casting director showcases, and Q & A sessions with successful folks in the industry. And most of them are completely free! Visit their website to check out how to sign up for the goodness.

SAG-AFTRA has a free online casting directory that's only available for its members.

You get to get your discount on. SAG-AFTRA members are eligible for hoards of discounts and deals on movie tickets, doctor visits, prescriptions, car rentals, real estate, legal services, and theater tickets. AND if you're an active, paid-up member, you get to vote for your favorites for the Screen Actors Guild Awards (it's my favorite time of the year when my mailbox is filled with a plethora of inspiring art and artists, and I actually get to pick my favorites!).

They help you make sure your work is legit. If you don't have an agent, you can check the SAG-AFTRA database to make sure the project you're working on is on the up and up. You can also call them and they'll let you know what's up as well.

You get a vote. If you're a union member, SAG-AFTRA encourages you to participate by voting on issues, joining a committee, or even serving on their board of directors or local council.

The SAG-AFTRA Foundation is a philanthropic 501(c)(3) non-profit organization that helps out its members with education and promotes children's literacy programs.

American Guild of Variety Artists

About AGVA: The American Guild of Variety Artists oversees mostly singers, dancers, performers, and stage managers in onstage productions including touring shows, theme park productions, circus folks, comedy shows, and lectures, public speaking events, and private and special events. It was founded in 1939 and is an AFL-CIO-affiliated labor union. For dancers, AGVA is the union for Rockettes and dancers in the Radio City Christmas Spectacular, dancers at most theme parks, dancers and performers in circus-style shows (Cirque du Soleil, etc.), and in event-based revue-style stage shows (think Vegas show gals). AGVA also governs (and co-represents alongside other unions) a few Broadway and many off-Broadway musical shows, tours, and regional productions.

Why to join:
AGVA, like its sister unions, negotiates and sets salaries for performers, makes sure employers uphold standards for breaks, rehearsal hours, and safe workplaces, and polices vacation time, sick pay, and overtime provisions. AGVA also takes excellent care of their members – the AGVA Sick & Relief Fund is a charitable and well-developed resource for any of its members that fall on hard times.

If you've always dreamed of being a Rockette, AGVA is the union for you and Radio City Music Hall is the place to be. AGVA is also a good union to consider if you have a special variety-type act that you want to promote and perform in places like late night talk shows, television competition shows, and private parties and special events. For instance, if you happen to be a pretty bad-ass stilt walker that has a whole moving tree act, AGVA is the place to go. (Incidentally, the stilt tree thing is totally in style at all of the fancy Los Angeles parties these days).

AGVA, like AEA, has union-only auditions for some of its contracts where union members are either the only talent that is permitted to audition, or they are the first performers to be seen at open auditions.

How to join:
If you have been offered a job that is under an AGVA contract, you may join the union. If you're working in one of the 25

right to work states, you don't have to join the union, but you definitely can (and might as well). When you get your contract from your employer, you'll also be given (or you should be given) an AGVA membership kit and application form that you need to fill out and send to the union to complete your membership.

AGVA is one of the only performing unions where you can petition to join without having an AGVA contract. You can send a resume listing your professional performing credits in your variety field to their membership department to be considered.

Responsibilities of membership:
AGVA doesn't take dues from your paycheck, but they bill you for it three times per year (April, August, and December). Dues is based on your earnings from performances and, according to their website in 2016, they're as follows:
$0-$4,999 - $72 annually
$5,000-$9,999 - $96 annually
$10,000-$14,999 - $132 annually
$15,000-$24,999 - $234 annually
$25,000-$34,999 - $540 annually
$35,000 or more - $795 annually

AGVA does have an initiation fee as well, but it's not listed on their website, and they are super secretive about it if you call and ask. According to my pals, it's around $1,000, but it can vary from contract to contract and employer to employer (if you're joining a new union on any contract, one good thing to get your agent to negotiate is to ask your employer to cough up your union initiation fee – no matter what union it is).

Benefits of membership:
Dancers (and other performers) that work under AGVA contracts can earn medical, dental, and vision coverage under the AGVA Welfare Trust Fund. The AGVA Welfare Trust Fund has a few different plans of coverage to choose from that require various amounts of work to qualify. For example, Plan A requires performers to accrue 15 days (or 3 consecutive weeks) of employment under an AGVA contract within a six-month period to meet eligibility requirements (Note that the employer must also be contributing to the Welfare Trust Fund on the performer's behalf.)

All of the plans are different, but they're all explained in pretty great detail on AGVA's website – www.agvausa.com

AGVA members that have been in good standing with the union for 5 or more consecutive years can continue to receive medical benefits even without continuing to work and without charge – check out Plan B on their website for more info

The AGVA Sick & Relief Fund is a resource for current and previous members that require emergency aid. They can pay for performers' bills (rent, utilities, phone) and give emergency grants. They also contribute to a ton of other performance-related charities like the Actor's Fund, the Phyllis Newman Women's Health Initiative, and many others.

American Guild of Musical Artists

About AGMA: The American Guild of Musical Artists represents most dancers in ballet and modern dance companies as well as dancers working under opera contracts (and opera singers and production personnel as well). AGMA was founded in 1936, is an AFL-CIO-affiliated labor union, and has approximately 8,000 members throughout the United States. AGMA is different than unions like SAG-AFTRA and AEA in that it doesn't prohibit its members from working non-union jobs so its members can work as much as possible in their field.

Why to join:

If you land a job as a dancer in one of the United States' leading dance companies, you'll be joining AGMA. If you're in a right-to-work state, you can opt not to join, but if you don't join up, you don't get to be part of the union party. And you'll want to. AGMA has the lowest initiation fees and dues of any of the talent unions, but they do just as much for their members as all of the other unions.

AGMA negotiates collective bargaining agreements for all of its members to make sure they have guaranteed salaries, maximum work hours, affordable health benefits, and vacation, sick, and overtime pay.

If you don't have a job in an AGVA company, it really doesn't make sense to shell out the dough to join up. This goes for all of the performing unions. If you don't think you'll ever work under a specific union's contract, it's a waste of time and money to be part of the union. It's kind of like paying for Netflix and not using it.

How to join:

Just apply! You can call AGMA's membership department to receive an application or to chat about specifics of joining. You can also download an application from www.musicalartists.org

Responsibilities of membership:

You've basically got to be bad ass nab an AGMA contract. AGMA signatories include companies like Alvin Ailey American Dance Theater, New York City Ballet, Martha Graham Dance, Joffrey Ballet, and Ballet Tech (amongst many other talented folks).

New AGMA members are required to pay a one-time initiation fee of $500, but you can wait a bit to pay it. The $500 bones is due when your income reaches $2,000 or within three years of your first AGMA contract date.

Yearly basic dues for AGMA are $78 per year due in your first week as an AGMA member and then by January 1st or each consecutive year.

AGMA members that are currently working must pay a working dues of 2% of their gross income from AGMA contracts (the 2% fee only applies to the first $100,000 – you don't have to pay dues on income over that). You can opt for AGMA to directly deduct your working dues or pay it on your own with a credit card or money order.

Benefits of membership:

You get health insurance! If you're a first time AGMA company member, your coverage will begin two months after your start date. AGMA members receive one month of health insurance for each month that their company shells over the monthly contribution dough on their behalf. (Dancers need to be on a weekly contract of 4 or more weeks for this benefit). If a dancer is contracted to work 20 weeks or more during a calendar year, the company must make health contributions for a full year (52 weeks). This protects dancers in companies that have extended layoff periods and do not have full-year seasons.

AGMA also has dental, vision, pension, and retirement plans that are available to its members.

You get a vote! AGMA is an entirely democratic union that's

completely run by its members, so every member in good standing gets a vote.

Discounts, discounts, and more discounts. AGMA members are eligible for discounts on car rentals, music and accessories, dancewear, dance studio rental, makeup, theater tickets, holistic health counseling, select restaurants, Pilates mat classes, prescription drugs, massage therapy, vocal lessons, and cruise vacations. Check out www.members.musicalartists.org for more specifics.

There are many other unions throughout the world that represent dancers. The unions above are the major players in the United States, though. One other union of note is ACTRA (the Alliance of Canadian Cinema, Television, and Radio Artists) which consists of more than 22,000 members that work professionally in Canada. Because Canada is so close to the United States and has a significant amount of performance work (both on camera and on stage), many dancers in America that are eligible decide to join ACTRA and pursue work in Canada. It makes sense - double the countries, double the employment opportunities!

AGENT'S TAKE: Many unions have different benefits, but that is precisely what they are - BENEFITS. It is tremendous to have unions that will provide health care, 401K plans and many other wonderful programs to assist union members. Most artists are independent contractors; therefore having the ability to belong to a union that can provide such opportunity will benefit and protect every artist that becomes a member.

In addition to the unions that protect and support working dancers, there is another organization of note that is affiliated with dance and the performing arts and is doing great things for the community:

The Actor's Fund

The Actor's Fund has been around for over 100 years helping our folks in the entertainment community. (CTFD is now a part of the ever-growing Actor's Fund). The Actor's Fund gives emergency financial assistance, care for elderly actors, affordable housing, career development assistance, and health care and insurance counseling. They have a career center, an assisted living facility, operate several affordable residences across the country, and do so much more for the community. They also operate the Al Hirschfeld Free Health Clinic that provides free health care to uninsured and underinsured professional dancers and performers.

    In short, when dedicated artists get together, they can do and create great things. I don't know many dancers that decide to pursue professional careers for the fame or the money; in fact, many dancers admit that they would be happy dancing for free if they didn't have to worry about paying bills. While that's a lovely sentiment, the dance community is all the better for the groups of people that are working every day to protect our rights, our health, and our artistic and intellectual property. If you ever meet a person that is working for any of the organizations above, take the time to thank them for their service and their dedication to making the professional dance community a better, safer, and more sustainable place.

7

Auditioning

Auditioning. This is probably the chapter to which most dancers skipped (if they didn't first skip to the agent section). Hey, skimmers, if you did skip to this chapter, welcome to the conversation! And good job in choosing wisely - you're correct in your enthusiastic quest for knowledge about all things audition - auditioning is very important, and everyone wants to know the magic secret of auditioning.

Unfortunately, I'm here to say that as far as I know, there is no magic secret to auditioning; no surefire way to ensure that people hire you to dance in a project (unless you're super loaded and you pay them to hire you, which is . . . well, bad ass. Live your life.) I believe the best and healthiest way to approach the act of auditioning is to control what you can control and leave the rest up to fate (or whatever you believe in). There are so many factors that go into getting a job that most dancers don't see. For instance, let's say you have a great audition for a commercial and are sure you have the job when you walk out of the room. Great job. And potentially, you DID have the job when you walked out of the room, but two days later, the budget of the commercial was cut by ten percent, and the producer decided to cut the group of dancers from nine to three. And the three folks that get the job are the producer's niece, the choreographer's assistant, and (since those two dancers happen to both be blonde women), a dark-complected man. Voila. You and your brilliant dancing have fallen off the table. And it's no fault of your own.

Here's the kicker: as a dancer, you'll rarely learn any of the things that happen after you leave "the room." Your phone will just stay sadly silent and you'll be left wondering what you did wrong. (Insert sad face emoji.) Multiply this scenario by a few auditions per week and anyone can see how frustrating this career can be. In this chapter, you'll read numerous audition tips and protocols, but the most important audition tip is the one that takes care of your soul.

Audition Tip: Don't take anything personally. I have had a motto of "do your best and leave it in the room" for many years. I recommend forgetting about an audition the minute you leave the room. Yes, you can learn some great lessons from reviewing what you did, what worked and what didn't, but by the time a dancer leaves an audition, they've already done that. Incessantly and obsessively picking apart every moment of an audition will make you crazy and is sometimes counter-productive to a dancer's self-confidence.

I understand that it can be hard to flip that mental switch to "off" (and even the suggestion of doing so is admittedly over-simplified), particularly in relation to projects that want to book more than others. And I'm in no way suggesting that dancers attempt to stop caring altogether. It's good to get excited! It's good to care! If you don't care about the outcome of an audition, then there's a pretty good chance that you're not so passionate about working as a dancer and would be better served to choose a different profession. If I have an audition that I get very excited about and then bomb, I give myself 4 hours afterward to do whatever I want to "mourn" it. I get ice cream, cry to my friends, drink a glass of wine or go punch it out in a boxing class. I let myself feel my feelings and then move on. Because, again, you NEVER know what happens behind the scenes. Just do your best in the moment and then move on.

There are so many facets to what to do in auditions, how to present yourself, how to stand out, etc. There are also exceptions to every suggestion and rule, so something that works for one particular person may not work for another. You have to find what works for you and what audition strategies fit your personality. Having said that, here are some general rules of thumb for being prepared and ready to book the jobs you want.

PREPARATION

Read everything. When you receive an audition notice from your agent, or you see a notice for an open call, make sure you read every little word of it. Every. Little. Word. Many a dancer has been caught unprepared in an audition because they didn't see, for instance, that somewhere in the paragraph of instructions was a directive to bring tap shoes. Or that the producer is only looking for dancers that can twirl a fire baton. Make sure to check dates as well. Most audition notices include a list of all of the dates that they plan to hold auditions as well as rehearsal and performance dates. If you have another project planned or a vacation on the books, make sure that you're available for ALL of the audition and performance dates before you attend the audition. There is nothing worse than booking a gig and then having to tell the producers that you can't do it because you didn't know you weren't available.

Overpack. You should approach packing for an audition in the opposite way that you would approach packing for a vacation. You can never have too many options. When preparing your bag(s) for auditions, bring a few clothing options, a few headshot options, and as many shoe options as you can tote. Pack water and snacks. If you sing, bring along some sheet music. Bring makeup, hair products, first aid options, any medication you might need, and (my favorite) a great attitude. All of these things are relevant in an audition situation, and I have seen all of them, at different times, be important to auditioners. ***Let's say you find yourself at a 3-hour audition for a musical theatre workshop, you haven't been given a break, and you forgot to eat breakfast. Or the casting director suddenly comes into the room and announces that the version of Chicago you'll be auditioning for is now reimagined, has a vaudevillian feel, and the choreographer requests that dancers do not wear black. In either of these situations, if you've prepared, you have a leg up on your fellow dancers. (And don't be stingy – if someone needs a band-aid and you have one, spread the love. Remember – it's a very small industry).

Research. If your agent calls (or emails) with an audition, do your research. First, READ your audition information and then use your favorite internet browser to glean as much additional information as possible. Look up the choreographer of the project for which you're auditioning and watch videos of his or her past projects. Look up the producer(s) and the director(s), and find other people that have previously worked for them. If you have friends that have worked for or auditioned for these folks before, ask them about their experience! If you ask a friend and they tell you, "I have auditioned for Rob Ashford three times before. Be prepared to stay a long time, stretch your hamstrings, and you'll probably do some partnering at the callback". That's valuable information! You can change your dentist appointment, stretch your hamstrings, and scope out the strongest and most coordinated-looking man in the room. Knowledge is power. Always.

Dress the part. Showing up looking the part is part of the battle. While some people in an audition may have a lot of experience and imagination, why tempt fate? If an audition notice says they're looking for "sexy biker chicks," don't try to show your versatility by showing up in a leotard and tan tights. I understand that everyone wants everyone else to know that they do everything, but attending an audition inappropriately dressed for the project can either make a producer think you're not intelligent or you are not willing to play by the rules. Both of these are probably likely to not get you hired. ***Additionally, please dress to dance. Go to an audition wearing clothing you might wear to a dance class (of that dance style), not a costume. Costumes, from the other side of the table, reek of desperation. Meaning, "Oh my gosh, look at that woman dressed in a leopard print thong leotard and cat ears – does she really think that will get her the job?" When in doubt, less is more. However, I have seen a costume work, but only when the dancer is truly fabulous. And they're often called back in spite of their crazy attire and rarely because of it.

*** A note on the importance of research and image in an audition: If you're auditioning for a new Broadway show choreographed by Susan Stroman, take five extra minutes to put your hair in a French twist and slap on some lipstick and eyelashes. If you have been living under a rock and didn't know who this Stroman lady is, please do your research. You'll see that most of her female dancers look like glamorous, leggy dancing Barbies. You think you don't look like a Barbie in real life? Well, do your best impression of one or call your agent to confirm that they're cool with non-Barbie-looking auditioners.

Are you a guy going in for a Justin Bieber video? Do the research on YouTube, accept the likely possibility that you might have to be shirtless, do some pushups, and subtly use some NOT-GLITTERY makeup to shade and define your assets. No lie, I watched a very talented dancer lose a lucrative gig as a replacement dancer on a cruise ship because the producer decided that he was "too chunky to look great without a shirt." That was the ONLY reason he was not offered a job that day. Again, if "guy-next-door-cute-chunky-dude" is your brand, rock it! There are tons of jobs for everyone, but don't LOSE a job because you didn't research and look your best.

Trick out your resume. This does NOT mean "make things up." NEVER lie, fabricate, or exaggerate on your resume. They will know. More on that later. What you should do, though, is include the credits that are relevant to the job you're auditioning for. If you are auditioning for a company, list your concert work first at the top of the resume. If you're auditioning for a TV gig, switch up your resume and put your on-camera experience at the top. If you have special skills that are specifically asked for in the audition notice, highlight them or put them in bold at the beginning of your special skills so they're evident. Sometimes casting folks take a quick glance at the first few things on a resume, and if they're not your most impressive or most relevant credits, you may be overlooked.

One of the many, many reasons not to lie on your resume is that the world of dance is very, very small. If a producer is not familiar with a dancer and is interested in them, chances are, they will peruse their resume. They'll look for a credit in which they know some of the players and do one of two things. Either they'll do a little background check on the dancer via someone they know that worked on one of the credits on your resume or they will ask the dancer in the room about the experience. For instance, "Oh, I loved that show. Such-and-such is a great choreographer. Who directed that tour again?" Side-side note: If it is on your resume, you MUST be able to spit out all of the key players at a moment's notice. If you are asked the name of one of these key players in an audition and you cannot remember, it may be detrimental to your job-getting chances. From a person-behind-the-table's standpoint, if you can't name one of the key players in one of the jobs you've listed, you either A) Lied on your resume that you did the project, B) Didn't care enough to remember the name of the person in question, or C) Cave under pressure when having to come up with something on the fly. None of these things speak well to your character, intelligence, or work ethic.

AGENT'S TAKE: Every audition will be different, therefore the more you audition the more confident you will be in making adjustments during one. Do your research on the project; the team attached to the project and the specifics of the audition. Arrive early with a positive outlook, fresh presentation, and tremendous skills. From the moment you arrive in the parking lot of the audition, you will be watched for your behavior, the energy you radiate, and the skills you present.

AUDITION BASICS

- **(Be a grown up and) Be on time.** While this shouldn't have to be stated, it apparently does because I have witnessed offenders to this rule on numerous occasions. Please always show up NOT on time, but early. If your dog died and you happen to HAVE to be late, enter quietly and apologize as you enter the room for your intrusion. Do not approach anyone – they're already busy running or teaching their audition – this will just add fuel to the fire. Just join the group learning the combination and cross your fingers that they don't remember later that you were the one that was tardy.

- **Look around you.** When you arrive (on time) to an audition, assume that everyone else in that vicinity is auditioning with you. Be courteous and make sure that when you check in, you don't usurp another person that has been patiently waiting their turn. Same thing goes for the audition room. I have seen more than one person almost bleed out and have to go via ambulance to the emergency room for stitches (only a slight exaggeration) because some overly-enthusiastic newbie kicked them in the head. Thinking of not heeding my advice in a crowded audition room (i.e. "screw it, I'm getting this job whether these bitches get out of my way or not")? Think again. They're always watching. Whether it sounds like a horror movie or not, the choreographer, director, and producers (and their assistants) are watching everything that happens in an audition room. Including and particularly how you treat others.

- **Assume that everyone is always watching.** In the same vein as the previous tip, you should always assume that people are always watching you in an audition. If you become discouraged, don't show it. If there is a spare moment, go over the combination rather than talking. If you don't like something, keep smiling and bitch to your friends about it later. Whatever you do, keep a positive and cooperative attitude at every point because they ARE watching you.

When I'm "behind the table", I like to get to an audition early and sit incognito in the waiting area beforehand. This is a great way to get to know the real personalities of dancers. As stated in the networking chapter, kindness and a collaborative spirit go further than technique any day. Again, just be a good human, please. Additionally, assume that you're being watched when learning a combination. A lot of directors and producers like to sit in the room while dancers are learning the combo. This is a great time to catch their eye. If the choreographer, when teaching, adds a movement that you know you will excel at (and you have the space and time), try it. You know that you're going to be awesome at, say, that pencil turn, but when they see you try it and succeed, they'll be more likely to keep an eye on you as the day progresses. Just don't do the whole combo show-off-style. That's an immediate turn-off.

AGENT'S TAKE: Artists train many years, therefore as you approach an audition know that you have done the work to prepare to the best of your ability. There are many reasons why a production team hires a particular artist for their project; therefore do your best in the audition and allow them to decide if what you have to offer is right for that particular opportunity. You may not book the job you audition for, however, if you make a positive impression, production will certainly consider you for their next project for which you might be a perfect fit.

WINNING THE ROOM

- **Tell a story.** No matter what the audition is, what the choreography is, or what the project is, you should always be telling a story when you dance. From auditioning for Taylor Swift's new tour to dancing for Hamilton to pirouetting for Nutcracker, you should always be telling a story. When dancers audition, very few of them tell a compelling story. Trust me; I've been behind the table numerous times. Look at it this way. Every dancer is (or should be) doing the same choreography in an audition, right? And let's say a particular audition is an agent call, so all of the dancers in the room are very adept at executing the choreography. Let's also assume that the production is looking for a specific type of dancer, so the room is full of, say, men that are roughly the same height, race, build and look. How does one behind the table choose the best man for the job? Well, they either hire their friends (see Chapter 3 – networking) or they (most often) choose the best storyteller. The more specific and complex your story is in an audition, the better. I love to place an imaginary person somewhere in the front of the room, choose how I feel about this imaginary person (appropriate to the gig and the choreography), and then find places in the choreography to play. Nine times out of ten, this will distinguish you from other dancers and make you a significantly more interesting performer. Note: I never will say that any approach will get you the job. This section is called "Winning the Room" not "Getting the Job". Again, you cannot control whether you get the job.

- **Work transitions.** As dancers, we have learned combinations in sets of eight since we were (probably) three or four years old. Something in a dancer's brain tends to stop when eight counts are over. Additionally, if a choreographer teaches the combination in sections, guess where most dancers blank out on what's next. Yep. Right after one of those sections. Or before. One of the most useful things you can do for yourself is to mentally or physically drill those transitions in the down-time of your audition. Not having to worry about what's next frees up your brain for even more elaborate and engaged storytelling which, in turn, makes you more LIKELY to get the job.

- **It's all in the details.** If a choreographer gives a correction or specifies something about a movement when teaching it, it's very, very important that you listen to this detail and implement it. For instance, if a choreographer says that all five fingers of your hand should be together in front of your hip rather than holding your hip the old-school way, that's important to them! It's probably a detail that they like about their choreography or achieves a specific look that they want for the piece. I know some choreographers that will automatically cut a dancer from an audition if they don't pay attention to the specified details. Think about it. If a dancer is not able to take a correction in the audition room, they are more than likely not going to be able to implement notes from a dance captain when performing. This will, in turn, make the choreography look messy, imprecise, or just plain bad. Why would a choreographer want to hire a person that might make their work look bad? Answer: they wouldn't. Even if a choreographer's detail throws you off (weird arms on a pirouette) or is not organic to your personal movement style (head angles that you just can't seem to coordinate with the rest of your body), try to do it anyway. Chances are, if you're having a hard time, other people in the audition room are as well. You'll be much more respected by the creative team for trying something whole-heartedly and not successfully achieving it than not trying at all.

- **Use your guts.** Sometimes directors and choreographers ask dancers to do odd things in auditions. I remember a particular audition for the original Broadway cast of Spamalot where the dancers were asked to emulate animals while dancing. (A room full of showgirls mooing like cows was pretty entertaining). Perhaps Casey Nicolaw did this purely for his own personal enjoyment, but it's more likely that he did it to find out which dancers were willing to take a risk. Some projects require dancers to be willing to try new things, be creative or ridiculous in their performances, or just plain be willing to (safely) throw themselves around. For projects that require this kind of gutsiness, it is imperative that a choreographer to know they have the right dancer for the job. The best way to find out if a dancer is brave or creative is to ask them to show this in the audition. If you're not willing or able to, say, emulate a monkey while doing fouettés, then maybe this isn't your gig. Often, dancers are afraid to look ugly or not graceful, but if a choreographer is asking for it, they definitely want to see it, and if you have the guts to try it, you are going to be more likely to get the callback.

***A little personal guts story: In one particular audition in early 2005, I walked into a callback that had a strip of Marley-type floor that the casting assistants were spraying down with wood cleaner. The (now Emmy-winning) choreographer asked us all to attempt to run and slide down the strip of floor in a wide surfer-like position. In all honesty, it was pretty terrifying. Some dancers chose not to do it, and most dancers slid a bit, caught air, and landed on their bums. I was one of the dancers that whole-heartedly went for it, slipped, and had the bruises on my bum the next day to show for it. And what did I get for my bravery? I was offered a featured role in a major motion picture for which I'm still receiving residuals over ten years later. When I asked the choreographer in preproduction why he hired me even though I failed to slide down the length of the room, he laughed and said, "I wasn't looking for people to be successful. I was looking for people to go for it."

There is, obviously, a caveat to the advice to go for broke and use your guts in auditions. If there is ever a point at which you feel unsafe or that you might be seriously injured, you should consider tapping out. One audition is not worth ruining your career.

- **Know your worth.** The best way to look at an audition or a potential job opportunity is that a dancer is essentially solving a problem. The problem is that a specific production company needs to find dancers to carry out their vision of a specific project. When a dancer goes to an audition and they're talented and available and trustworthy, problem solved! The "people behind the table", as we often refer to them, are looking for dancers to be great when they walk into a room. The misconception is that those behind-the-table folks are "judging" dancers or waiting for them to mess up. Trust me; they don't have time for that. They just want their problem solved. And you're essentially their solution.

THE AFTERMATH

- **Let it go.** In the now-iconic words of Idina Menzel, let it go. As I stated earlier, give yourself a short amount of time to ponder your choices in the audition room and then move on to think about something more productive. It's also important from an outside image standpoint to move on. There is nothing more desperate-sounding than a dancer that keeps asking his friends and representation if they've heard if anyone was offered a specific job. And if you hear that someone else has been offered a job that you auditioned for, graciously congratulate them. "They must have only wanted tall dancers. I don't know why I even went" is both rude and can make the dancer that got the job feel like they didn't earn it fair and square (which they more than likely did).

- **Keep in touch.** If an audition went well, but you end up not booking the job, it can still be a win in your corner. Getting a callback or doing well at an audition is one great point of contact between you and the choreographer/director/producer. (Remember the seven points of contact from the networking chapter?). First of all, enter your audition date, who was there, how you did, and any other pertinent information to your handy contact spreadsheet. Then, if you have time and one of the people in the room is a contact you would like to keep, send a thank you note. It is not inappropriate to send a concise thank you note to a casting director for including you in the audition. Particularly if it's a smaller audition or a call for something more high-profile. And guess what? That's your second (or next) point of contact.

- **Keep fighting the good fight.** All information about how you perform in an audition is helpful and can help you grow as a dancer. If you had trouble with the combination because it was a bit too technical for you, get into ballet class. If you were winded by the time your group went up to dance, get in the gym. If you didn't have an outfit that was cute and comfortable, go shopping. We learn from our mistakes AND our successes. Make sure that when you're reviewing your audition, you take note of the things you did RIGHT. (As dancers, we tend to focus more on our corrections, what's wrong and can be fixed, or the negative aspects of our dancing rather than balancing it out with remembering the positive things about our dancing as well as the negative).

~

AGENT'S TAKE: Be present and focused. Be polite. Be ready to answer questions and speak to the production team in a clear and confident voice. Leave the negative and self-doubting at home - that will only hold you back. Be supportive of the other artists in the audition, as they will respond positively to your support and reciprocate in the same manner.

Respect the audition process, those who are providing the

opportunity and the ability to showcase your tremendous talent. When preparation meets opportunity with a positive approach you will gain experience, visibility and likely a wonderful job in the industry.

───⁂───

All in all, the most important thing to remember about an audition is just to do your best in the moment. That's all a choreographer or director can ask. You are not going to become a significantly better technician in the space of your one-hour audition, so chill. While nerves are a common and understandable part of auditioning, they really shouldn't be. There is nothing you can do in an audition room other than trying your best with your best attitude to work with whatever choreography you've been given. If that doesn't get you the job, then it wasn't meant to be, and you keep on keeping on.

8

Working

Great job. You've gotten a job. This chapter is all about how to do a good job . . . on the job. The way in which a dancer conducts him or herself on the job is one of the best indicators of if they'll be offered another. Many choreographers have a group of dancers that they bring with them from job to job – both because they've found dancers that are adept at executing their choreography and because they've found good humans that they like to work with. Your goal should be to become one of these people.

Navigating a new production can be tricky. Whether you're starting a new gig with a completely new cast or you're a replacement in an already-established company, there are some general rules of set and stage etiquette, respecting hierarchy, how to adjust to different circumstances, backstage courtesy, self preservation, and other things that are pretty handy to know before you start working.

Remember that the job offer is just the beginning of the journey. Once you have an offer, you must agree on a contract, be fitted into costumes, participate in studio and dress/tech rehearsals, work through shows or shoot days, and attend screenings and publicity-related social events. All the while, and very importantly, dancers need to remember to look out for themselves, their health, their well-being, and their personal reputation in the midst of what can be a whirlwind of activity and (sometimes) confusion.

No book can tell a dancer everything about working in the industry, but this chapter is a good start.

CONTRACTS

Regardless of what kind of dance job you attain, you should be offered a contract in writing before you start working. Sometimes for on-camera work, you're asked to sign the contract on the day of the shoot, but in general, you'll have it beforehand. *Note: If you are asked to participate in a paid project that does not have a contract available, you should be very suspect. Without a contract, you cannot guarantee your payment, the appropriate use of your likeness, and your safety and working conditions on set (just to name a few). In short, if you don't have a contract, ask for one or be willing to deal with consequences.

The first and most obvious thing you should do is to take the time to read your contract. Even if you're fortunate enough to have an agent to read and review your contract for you, you still should take the time to read it thoroughly. While a lot of dancers will state that they're "just happy to be working" and don't have any specific requests in a contract, read it anyway. You never know. Check the dates on your contract as well to make sure you don't have any vacations, weddings, or other non-negotiable events planned in the future that might conflict with a rehearsal or shoot date. The dates on your contract might be negotiable, but you have to READ IT FIRST. Also make sure to check any clauses about changing your appearance (I like to dye my hair on a whim, but under some contracts, that could get you fired). Oh, and be sure to double-check your pay rate. I know more than a few dancers that have been very surprised when they received their first paycheck (and by then, they were locked in to the pay rate on the contract they signed).

An important side note: Never ever discuss how much you're paid. With anyone. Unless you're on a favored nations contract (one where everyone is paid the same and it's public knowledge), you cannot assume that your fellow performers are bringing in the same dough as you are. Maybe you have a good amount of experience and the production team decided to pay you an extra $100/day, but they don't tell you. If you mention your rate to another dancer, they could potentially (and possibly angrily) go to your producers and demand the same pay. This is not cool for your relationship with the producers or with the angry dancer.

Lastly, be sure to keep a copy of your contract. Some contracts can be pretty lengthy – particularly long-term contracts with larger franchises or tours with music artists may include numerous very specific and sometimes eccentric clauses. It's always handy to have a copy of what you signed to check back in. "Is my per diem the same in Sydney as it is in Savannah?" is a question that many dancers don't think about until they're in month four of the tour and they arrive in Sydney. It's also helpful to keep the signed copy of the contract just in case any producers try to pull a fast one and say that you signed something that you didn't (don't worry – it rarely happens). On a personal side, I think it's fun to go into my filing cabinet, flip through all of my old contracts, and reminisce about past projects.

REHEARSALS AND FITTINGS

Every director and choreographer runs his or her rehearsals in a different manner. Some choreographers show up to rehearsal with a very specific plan, already-set choreography, and a good idea of how to go about realizing their vision. Other choreographers arrive to rehearsal with only an idea or two and then create from there. I will say that while preparation seems like the more efficient, I've found that no one approach is better than the other. I worked with a particular choreographer that walked into rehearsal, gave us a stack of photo books, asked us to translate the photos into movement to create a few counts of eight, and then left the room for a good half hour. When he returned, we showed him our choreography and he then artfully and expertly wove the phrases together to make a beautiful piece of choreography.

Your job as a dancer is to discern which way your director and choreographer prefer to interact with their dancers and then adapt your personal way of working to theirs. How do you learn this? Listen. Watch. And shut the heck up. Some creative team folks will ask for input like, "I need some sort of lift here. What do you guys think would work?". This is your opportunity to politely suggest (or better yet – SHOW) an option. Some directors and choreographers would prefer that their dancers do exactly what they ask and nothing more. This means that your first few days of rehearsal should be fairly silent ones. Do what you're told and do it well. And again, shut the heck up. Once you feel very familiar with the way rehearsal is conducted you can be a bit less circumspect and just enjoy. Incidentally, this is a great detail to put in your networking spreadsheet for potential future projects with your current creative team!

Here are a few do's and don'ts of rehearsal and fitting etiquette:

- **DO** – Write it down. After a full day of rehearsal (or during your breaks), I urge you to write down your choreography, blocking, and notes. And physically WRITE it down (don't type it) – dancers are generally inherently kinesthetic learners and the physical action of writing words is much more effective for memorization than typing. Every choreographer I know expects what they set the day before to be memorized and pretty close to perfect by the day after. This frees them up to move on with more choreography or blocking rather than re-teaching what they worked the day before. This means that you must do your homework. Write it down and rehearse it. Dance in your living room, get together with your buddies an hour before rehearsal, employ a visualization technique. Whatever you need to cement all of your new information in your brain, do it. It's great for your reputation and believe it or not, not every dancer does it. If you return with a pristine rendition of the previous day's work, your cleanliness and evident work ethic will not only get you noticed, it might also get you a solo or great placement in the coming days' choreography. If a choreographer can trust you to be awesome with their previous day's work, they can trust you to rock the following days as well.

- **DO** – Look nice. Yes, you have already gotten the job, but don't show up to rehearsal looking like you just rolled out of bed. A creative team wants to see the same people they hired in the audition show up in the rehearsal room. If you show up looking like a homeless Olson twin, the people that hired you might consider finding someone else. Looking nice does not necessarily mean false lashes, a manicure, and a DryBar blowout. Just use your common sense and present yourself in a professional manner. Also, you never know when a photographer will show up to take publicity shots for either the program, the "making of" book, or BTS (behind the scenes) video for the YouTube segment. Incidentally, this is also a good reason to always be up on your choreography – you don't want to be the one person that's on the wrong leg . . .

- **DO** - Bring provisions. Pack alternate dance shoes, a change of clothes, deodorant, knee pads, snacks, water, and any other things you think you may need during rehearsal. Particularly over pack if you're working on a project or with a creative team with which you're unfamiliar. I'm always thankful when I'm asked to do partnering after a super sweaty morning of dancing and I am able to change to dry dance clothes during a break. (Incidentally, my dance partner is generally thankful as well). This will also gain you points with your fellow dancers if someone happens to, say, forget deodorant, you are their favorite person if you have some to spare (preferably the spray kind).

- **DO** – Try anything once. Unless it's a crazy stunt or something completely inappropriate, if a choreographer or director asks you to do something, do it. If you're traveling from one place to another and you know you won't make it in the allotted time, the worst thing to do is speak up and say, "I'm not going to make it over there in that time". Sure, you may NOT be able to make it, but the same rules apply to rehearsal as do in acting improvisation. Dancers should always strive to say, YES . . . AND. "Yes, I'd love to try that" is awesome. So, you try it and it doesn't work a few times, it looks weird, and the choreographer changes it. The "trying it" approach has the same outcome as speaking up before trying it, but in the former, you get brownie points from the choreographer for being a team player.

- **DO** – Be a problem solver. This is a tricky thing to do because there is a very fine line between being a problem solver and making suggestions that aren't wanted, so proceed with caution when actively attempting to problem solve in the rehearsal room. Ask yourself if your solution to a perceived problem that the choreographer has will change the aesthetic of the piece or just behind-the-scenes make things easier. If your solution makes things easier on anyone (including principals, your fellow dancers, your prop people, etc.), wait until a lull in the action, raise your hand (yes, like in school), and make your suggestion. One appropriate problem solution is: "I can grab that costume piece that Such-and-Such Singer just dropped because I'm exiting that way at that time anyway". Another possibility is: "Sally Dancer isn't making it to her spot on time. I can cut upstage rather than going left to leave her a path. Does that make it easier?" Creative teams love having their problems solved by a dancer that's a team player. They also don't love being interrupted with a suggestion that is not relevant or useful for what they're trying to achieve. If you'd consider yourself a newbie to working in dance or a newbie to working in a particular genre or dance venue, the safest thing to do is to keep your suggestions to yourself and listen and learn.

- **DO** – Love everything. Or if you don't love it, zip it. This is particularly important in your costume fittings. If you don't happen to like the unflattering shading of your body suit, then, well, nobody cares. It's not your job to costume yourself. Same thing with wigs. If you don't like your wig, wear it anyway and smile. If they ask your opinion, that's a different story, but unwanted comments from the dancer peanut gallery can start a train of gossip grumble that can get a young dancer on anybody's bad side quickly.

One caveat to this love fest is that if you are given a costume, shoe, wig, or other apparatus (snake, maybe) that is going to hinder your performance in any way, gently ask about it. The key word is ASK. Make sure to raise your arms and do a few battements to make sure that you can move the way you will be expected to move in the project. Pirouette in your shoes and jump around a bit to make sure everything fits perfectly.

If doesn't, an appropriate way to address an issue goes something like this: "I raise my arms in this piece a lot (demonstrate not being able to raise arms). Is there a way that I might be able to get a little more room to move?" Make sure you then follow this with something like, "But these sleeves are super cool". The more a costume designer likes you, the cooler costume you get (sometimes). Familiarity breeds preferential treatment whether we want it to or not. However, it's important not to settle with ill-fitting shoes or a costume piece that you even think might be painful or eventually cause injury. One little "it'll be fine" thing multiplied by eight shows per week . . . well, multiplies. Plantar fasciitis, anyone?

This "loving everything" suggestion also applies to your (and everyone else's) choreography. Execute your choreography to the best of your ability and trust that the director or choreographer will change it if it looks bad. Don't ever dance choreography poorly in hopes that it will be changed. Everyone can see straight through that ploy and you run the risk of just being seen as less talented than you are (incidentally, this passive aggressive behavior happens more often in the rehearsal room than you think). The same rules apply to choreography, though. If you're asked to do something that you're not comfortable with or that may cause injury, gently discuss it with your choreographer. If this isn't successful and you still feel strongly about it, call your agent. You only get one body in this life and my advice is to not screw it up permanently for just one gig.

- **DO** – Hang out. If the cast goes out after rehearsal and invites you along, go for it! Dinner or drinks after a long day can help you get to know your fellow dancers (and creative team) and relationships are always key in this industry. But DON'T get wasted. If you are imbibing alcohol, set a hard limit before you go out. There is nothing worse than a sloppy coworker. More importantly, you never want to give anyone (creative team or fellow dancers) an excuse to think you're ever doing anything other than your 100% best in the rehearsal room. Hangovers included. If your coworkers see that you're responsible enough to be moderate (or abstain) with your substances, they will associate that with your responsibility and reliability in work as well.

- **DON'T** - Please don't change anything you don't like without telling (or, better yet, asking) anyone. Even little things. They will notice. Don't cut the band off of the top of your tights because you think it gives you muffin top. Don't restyle your wig because it falls in your face. And heavens to Betsy, please don't subtly change choreography or blocking because you think your version is more flattering to you. Every now and then, it works, but if it doesn't, you can get busted pretty quickly. The whole forgiveness/permission rule rarely works in rehearsal and I've seen dancers that were let go for less.

- **DON'T** – Strong perfumes and body oils are highly discouraged in rehearsal. Unless you're in NYCB and Mr. Balanchine has expressly chosen you a signature fragrance, step away from the Chanel No. 5. Some folks are allergic to some scents and if you happen to be working on a musical, many singers are vehemently averse to perfumes. A sensible shower and deodorant is all you need. (Incidentally, this should go without saying, but please bathe on a regular basis – I have heard many a nasty word passed around the rehearsal room about a dancer or two that has failed to uphold olfactory standards.

- **DON'T** – Name-dropping is one of the least attractive things a dancer can do. I get it – you are new to a group of people and an environment and you want to let them know that you are worthy of being part of the project. Trust me, if you've toured with every major music artist, your fellow dancers will either already know that (thanks, Google) or they will eventually find out when they read your bio. Resist the urge. It's always obvious to everyone within earshot when a person attempts to name-drop, ever how sly they might be. And, even more, if you don't know what all of your fellow dancers have done, you always run the risk of being out-name dropped. For instance, "I remember the last time I had this many lifts was when I did Justin Beiber's last tour. It was just plain rude", says Dancer 1. "I saw that tour. That's when Justin and I had just started dating. So many lifts", says Dancer 2. Or even worse, "You think it was rude? Wow. I'll tell my cousin. He was the choreographer". Strong and silent wins the prize.

- **DON'T** – Have inappropriate relations with your coworkers. The more crass phrase also applies: Don't sh#! where you eat. Dancers are generally very physical folks who think nothing of randomly picking each other off the ground, laying on top of one another backstage, and giving impromptu back massages during breaks. While, on an official level, this is still inappropriate behavior, these actions are also part of the dance culture. Having intercourse or making out with any of your fellow coworkers, including and most importantly the creative team and/or music artists, is a really, really bad idea.

  ***First of all, if you are inappropriate with a coworker, there is always the potential that the next day at work will be completely awkward and you will be distracted from your dancing. There's also the possibility that some sort of relationship is sparked, it ends quickly (and potentially not amicably), and then you're at odds with one of your fellow dancers (and probably a few of his or her friends) for the duration of the contract. If you've done the dirty with someone from behind the table, it's a likely possibility that that person won't hire you again (either out of embarrassment of an evening of poor choices or to protect themselves from the possibility that you might want more (stalkers, anyone?). Then there's the perception that the rest of your coworkers might form of you. If you're shacking up with a music artist or producer/director/choreographer, you will more than likely gain a reputation for "sleeping your way to the top" (though that rarely happens in the business –

the "casting couch" is a rare thing these days). And if it's just Jill or Joe Schmo dancer with whom you've made poor choices, you might just be seen as loose. While we currently live in a modern world and it's a bit antiquated to advise one to keep one's underwear on, you never know. There are plenty of other pebbles on the beach. And they usually have cuter feet.

AGENT'S TAKE: There are many artists that are terrific dancers, however, do not handle the business end of booking work quite as well. Be well rounded in your creative skills as well as your business skills. If you have questions about a project, ASK (especially before you sign the contract.) In situations where you are not clear or unhappy, make sure to ask the appropriate individuals (agent or production manager) in a tone that is not defensive. Individuals are more likely to help find a positive resolution when approached in a fair, reasonable, and professional manner. Attack mode does not get you very far and does not bode well with those that you approach in such manner. There is a big difference between inquiring positively to find a resolution and relentless negative venting. Be professional and you will likely find positive results.

PERFORMING

You've made it. You have put in the time in the rehearsal room and now you've arrived on set or at the theatre and you're ready to rock and roll (or revoltade). First things first, anybody that is earning a paycheck dancing in any venue is one of the very lucky few. Whatever you do, remember that it is an absolute privilege to be chosen to dance and get paid to do so and there are thousands of people that would burn all of their La Ducas to take your place. Be grateful, gracious, and above all, thankful. If you find yourself wanting to bitch about little things, you should probably consider choosing another profession or do some serious journaling at home.

Working as a professional dancer is a coveted and difficult career and, to be honest, it should be an honor.

- **Arrive** – You never get a second chance to make a first impression and while it may seem after numerous rehearsals that you've known all of your coworkers forever, when you arrive to a theatre or set for the first time, you're probably doubling your number of coworkers. If you're working on stage, you'll be meeting all of the lighting folks, prop folks, sound folks, electric folks, ushers, house managers, etc. for the first time. If you're on set, you'll be meeting your assistant directors, gaffers, sound operators, script supervisors, production assistants, and maybe extras and principals for the first time. Treat your arrival as you would your first day of rehearsal – tread with caution. Be polite. Repeat everyone's name and attempt to commit it to memory and remember that you still LIKE EVERYTHING. If you arrive on set and immediately start complaining to your 2nd AD that rehearsals are a disorganized mess, you'll probably not make a great first impression. Particularly if the 2nd AD has worked with this particular director numerous times . . . and enjoyed it.

- **Everyone is important** – If a person is on set or backstage in a theatre, they're there to do an important job. Don't be that dancer that's too cool to talk to the PA (production assistant) or the child wrangler (the person in charge of making sure any minors in a production stay safe and make it to their places on time). First of all, from a human standpoint, humans are humans are humans and should be treated as such. From a business standpoint, it's a good chance that PA and child wrangler are budding producers and directors and will one day, probably sooner than later, be in the position to return your kindness. Use your spreadsheet from chapter 3 to remind yourself of people's names, job descriptions, hobbies, and contact information. If you've left a Broadway show where you've sent Tom the spot operator a birthday card or remembered to ask about his hot rod renovation, he will be more likely to give your friends a backstage tour.

- **Find your direct report** – If you need to know where the restroom is, you do not want to be asking the director on a set during a shot. One of the first things you should do upon arriving to a set or stage is to figure out your go-to person if things go down. Generally if you're performing on stage, it's a stage manager, stage manager's assistant, or dance captain and if you're on set, it can be the 2nd AD (assistant director) or choreographer's assistant. BUT every set is different. Shooting a new Todrick Hall video will be a very different experience than putting up a national tour of a musical, so ask the first person that takes charge of showing you where to go who this person should be. And more importantly, remember their names. Both the person greeting you and your direct contact.

- **Be careful** – Yeah, yeah, we've all heard it. Stages and hot sets are dangerous places and we should always be circumspect when dancing (or walking) on them. I'm here to tell you that these things are very, very deadly end-your-career true. There are teams and teams of people that are dedicated solely to making sure that dancers (and actors) are safe when they're working, but accidents do happen. I have seen people fall through trap doors above prosceniums, lean against flats and shatter glass above their heads, and step on probably hundreds of nails and construction equipment.

***The most important prevention technique for accidents on stage and set is awareness. Keep your eyes and ears open. If there is a jib, make sure you know where it is at all times so you don't accidentally punch or run into it (if you don't know what jibs are, look them up – they're pretty cool). If you're on a stage and there are moving set pieces, identify a way off of them if they happen to start moving when they're not supposed to. And never, wherever you are, walk anywhere in the complete dark. Ask a stagehand for a flashlight or a dresser for a bite light or just plain freeze and tell someone that you can't see.

This point of advice deserves its own paragraph because

dancers are notorious for not following it. Here goes: Wear. Shoes. I know, we don't like to. And yes, if you're doing a music video on a green screen that is set in the desert or performing a contemporary piece on stage, you will not be wearing shoes when performing, but bring slippers and keep them close by. Sets can change from day to day. I have seen a sound stage be an apartment one day and a subway station the next. This means that there are nails, glue, glass, and other potentially dangerous materials CONSTANTLY on the ground just waiting for your very precious feet to walk over them. Likewise, I have seen more nails sticking out of the ground on Broadway stages than anyone could ever imagine. Just wear shoes. Please? Make it a fun weird you-ism. Maybe you're the fun dancer with the kooky bunny slippers, but take an extra moment to preserve your career and rock those bunnies.

- **Be present . . . always** – It is to your advantage to consistently remain present during the entire shoot/performance (and tech) process. It's tedious, but it is crucial. Shoot days can last into the double digits of hours (my longest was 20 hours – 6am until 2am at a bowling alley in Queens), so the temptation to check your phone, goof off with other folks, or just plain zone out is always present. The same thing applies to the stage. During tech week, try to be in the house (in the seats of the theatre) at all times when you're not on the stage and make sure that if you're in your dressing room that your monitor is up and you have one ear toward what's going on at all times.

    You never know when the director is going to say, "I need an extra person dancing in this section", and if you've been listening to what she/he has been saying, you can be the first to volunteer. If you're on stage, tech week can be very slow and then it can, without any notice, move very quickly. Don't be the dancer they page on the intercom to come to the stage because you're outside face timing with your boyfriend. And definitely don't be the dancer in one of the boxes with their headphones in watching porn that's been downloaded on the company wifi (true story).

The most important aspect of remaining present takes place during a performance. Obviously, nobody wants to miss an entrance, so if you're doing a long-running show and you're catching up on season three of House of Cards between numbers, just use only use one headphone and make sure not to miss your cues. This is another reason to be friendly with your fellow castmates. If people like you, they'll let you know when something is coming up. If they don't, well, you're on your own. If you're on the other side of the attention spectrum and you see a dancer that is in danger of missing a cue, please do the humane thing and wake them out of their stupor.

This should go without saying (but I'll touch on it anyway), but please also always remain mentally and physically present when you are actually performing on set and on stage. First of all, again, dancing can be a little dangerous. I've seen a dancer crack another dancer's cheekbone with a character heel and I've seen a gentleman miss catching his partner's leg and drop her. It's important to physically be there, but mental presence is key, as well.

Remaining mentally present can get difficult the thirteenth time you run the same 30 seconds of dance to shoot for a film or the 245th show on your second revolution around the globe with a music artist. It's so important to genuinely connect with your fellow dancers and notice if they're "in it to win it" or if they need a little encouragement. Great team-playing dancers are good at noticing when their castmates need a little wink, a goofy "yee haw", or an extra bit of physical partnering energy or love onstage. You must remember that energy is not a finite resource. If you share your joy with another, it compounds. And when you do, it generally makes both of your performances more genuine and more joyous (or sexy or fierce – whichever you are going for).

- **Tell a new story** – Performing for extended periods of time can be exhausting and it's tempting to "phone it in" every now and then. Dancers, you should remember that every audience is seeing you dance for the first time. And if they aren't and they're seeing you the second or third time, then it's all the more important to tell a slightly different story every time you do a show. Likewise, if you're on set and you're doing the same one or two minutes of choreography ten to twenty times, you need to bring it every time. Including the first time. If a director says they're going to roll on rehearsal, this is not your opportunity to mark. Sometimes the rehearsal take ends up in the cut and if you're doing a half-ass job, you'll be sad when you go to the premiere or see it online.

If you've gotten far enough to be performing, you probably know this already, but every dance piece tells a story. Whether you've been expressly given one by the creative team or not, you are telling some kind of story with your body. If you can entertain yourself (and hopefully your audience) with as specific or a story as you can imagine, it makes you instantly one of the most interesting things on the stage or camera lens. If you've been telling the same story for a while, switch it up slightly. Find new people on stage to relate to, change your imaginary location, choose a new word that is your theme word for that specific take or performance. Changing the word that's going through your mind from, say, "enticing" to "animalistic" will definitely switch up your approach to your performance. Just make sure that your internal changes are still in keeping with the integrity of the piece. If you're a dancer in a national tour of the musical *Oklahoma*, choosing "trashy-sexy" is potentially not the best option. If you're shooting a Robin Thicke music video, it's probably the perfect phrase.

- **Respect the privacy of the set/stage** – Let's say you've just arrived on set for a television show, you've been given your call sheet and met the 2nd AD, and you've been escorted to your trailer and told to hang out for a bit. You look down at your call sheet and see your name!!! Your name is on an official television call sheet! And not only is your name on an official television call sheet, your name is right next to Tina Fey and Jimmy Fallon! You've officially made it! And your first inclination is probably to share the information with your friends! You take a pic of the call sheet and post it to your social media. Guess what? That can get you fired IMMEDIATELY!

First of all, many call sheets have sensitive information on it like cell numbers, emails, cast, and the location of shoot. Do you think that if you were a crazy Tina Fey fan and you saw that she was shooting in a restaurant in Palo Alto that you might try and show up on set? What can happen is a crazy fan stampede and if anyone finds out that Dancing Bartender #2 caused it, you're probably done. And what about contact information? Seriously, you do not want to be the person that shared Jimmy Fallon's cell number with the world. Additionally, you don't want to be the person that shared any producer or director's contact information with anyone either – "can I get a job" emails and calls will ensue. Trust me. And what if the episode you happen to be on is a surprise episode and the network hasn't announced that the television show you are on will have a musical episode? If you've social media'ed anything about your show, you've outed the network's surprise. Doesn't bode well for future employment. Likewise, if, for example, you are the first person to post costume photos on your personal social media from the new production of Troop Beverly Hills the musical and Broadway.com gets a whiff of it, you've taken the wind out of the sails of your production's PR firm's planned costume segment on Good Morning America.

The long and the short of it is that you should never post any photos from set (or from a new stage production) before either the episode/film/music video airs or the show opens. This includes photos of your costumes, makeup, photos with cast members, or even text that includes anything about what you're doing. I know it's hard and you are probably very excited to be part of an awesome production, but if you tease your appearance on your social media, it's just as fun. Things like, "On set today for a super exciting project! More details to come!" can satisfy a little of that need to share with the world.

Having said that, DO take photos, but save them for AFTER. A great photo next to a famous person on set or in a fun costume is great for your social media following, your imdb list of photos, your gallery on your personal website, and your general street cred. Just make sure that you are discreet, you do not interrupt any of the action (do all documenting during breaks), and that you ask first before snapping away.

- **Be a good roommate** – If you're not one of the very lucky very few, you'll probably be sharing a dressing room with one or more people. I cannot stress enough that you should be courteous in every way in your dressing room space. Everyone prepares differently for a performance. Some people need to silently focus and mentally prepare while they do hair and makeup and others like to play loud rap music and dance around like they're at an 80's rave. If you're one of those loud music folks, get yourself a pair of wireless headphones. If you're one of those quiet-types, get yourself some earplugs. The moral of the story is to conform to the culture of the dressing room.

AGENT'S TAKE: Remember to pack your patience. Not everyone will be as tidy as you are, or they may do things you find completely odd. However, finding a balance and making it work will bring you and your roommate peace. Understand that you will need to compromise at times, and being flexible in rooming and dressing room situations will make the process much more bearable.

If you're a replacement in a show, dressing room politics are even more precarious. Consider that if you're joining a dressing room already-in-progress, they might have some protocol already in place. Some may be silly and some just plain weird, but go with it. When I joined my first Broadway show as a replacement, my job was to take the bag of sweaty chorus girl underwear down to the laundry. No joke. I was told, "The new girl always carries the coo bag". As gross as it was, it was my sort of initiation into the team and my gracious willingness to jollily comply helped ingratiate me in the group of ladies who had been doing the show together (some for as many as seven years). Likewise, if you notice that the person you're replacing always plays rochambeau before they go onstage in act two, add it to your tracking notes and continue the tradition. These examples of "team player" gestures will go a long way and will help you to ingratiate yourself into a new group of individuals. Particularly if you're a replacement that's replacing a person that was well-loved or very popular, I would recommend adapting yourself as seamlessly to the already-well-oiled machine of your new show as possible. Don't worry – you'll make your own impression in time.

Another important thing to do in a dressing room is to keep your space relatively tidy. Some dressing tables have lines marked between spaces (unions have rules for how small/large a dressing space must be). Make sure you keep your crap inside these lines! If there aren't lines, create your own mental space and do not exceed it.

Some of my best friendships in the world have started in dressing rooms and they can be a place of honest commiseration, joyous and raucous celebrations, and just plain strength in numbers. Walk into a dressing room of any project expecting to find your new best friends. If this doesn't happen, it doesn't happen, but positivity goes a long way. If there happens to be a bad apple or two in your midst, the best way to go is to refuse to engage in negativity. This does not mean that you refuse to engage at all, you should just lightly change the subject, make a self-deprecating or silly joke, or feign having to use the restroom. People will eventually get the idea. While negative experiences can come about in the dressing room, for the most part, dressing rooms are a home base for roving artists, a fiercely loyal den of sister or brotherhood, and places that will be backdrops for numerous fun and precious memories.

- **It's not all fun and games** – While you definitely want to create great relationships with your new coworkers and play along with their fun backstage and dressing room antics, please make sure you don't go too far. Sure, it's absolutely fine to do a quick hammer dance with the stage right prop guy after you exit the stage, but some pranks (particularly ones that happen onstage) can go too far. There's a story that by now has become Broadway lore about a woman in Les Miserables that would subtly toss her fake baby off of the top of the barricade when she faced upstage. The cast and crew found it to be hilarious until one evening her (apparently very heavy) baby hit their Eponine in the head and knocked her unconscious. You can guess someone was written up for that little escapade.

AGENT'S TAKE: Be careful to not cross the line into unprofessional. In the midst of having fun, remember to take a step back to avoid any misunderstanding that could jeopardize your position.

Performers often like to push the boundaries of appropriateness onstage, particularly in long-running shows and tours. I remember games of "pass the cocktail weenie" during the Ascot Gavotte in My Fair Lady and gentlemen that would hide their cell phones up their sleeves during Act 1 or The Nutcracker. My advice on all of these antics is to politely smile, enjoy your coworkers' brashness, and step away. Trust me, it's never worth potentially losing your job to participate in an onstage game of "find the blind villager" during the mob scene of Beauty and the Beast. Seriously, if you're that bored with your job, I'd recommend getting into a few auditions and finding a new one.

- **Greet your adoring public** – If you're a newbie, you probably can't imagine why anyone would not want to sign autographs after a show. I mean, that's what we all dream of as little kids, right? You finish your performance and walk out of the stage door to greet a cheering mass of adoring fans. Then you commence artfully signing your name on programs as flashbulbs blind you and people shout your name. Right? Or was that just me? Either way, if you're on the stage or screen for any period of time, you will attract a fan or two (or thousands) and the manner in which you interact with them can be a huge factor in your career.

AGENT'S TAKE: Be respectful to those who appreciate your talent. Isn't this one of the things you worked for hard for? Be a mentor to young artists by being gracious that they admire you and your work.

First, let's address the laziness factor. Signing autographs after a show and/or responding to fan mail or fan messages on social media takes a relatively small amount of time. If these people have taken the time out of their lives to contact you, then a response obviously means a lot to them. You should consider it part of your job to respond to fans. It is your job to exit the stage door and politely greet and briefly speak to people that would like to speak to you. If you've ever been a young dancer looking up to someone on television or on a stage, then you should get it. Not to get too heavy about it, but you're inspiring the artists of the future. It takes an extra 15-20 minutes at most and will help your social media AND your soul. If, for some reason, your house is on fire and you cannot stay to greet your adoring public, please find a discreet exit from the venue that will (hopefully) not take you past the public. And if you do run into folks and you cannot spend the time with them, apologize politely that your house is on fire, smile, wave, and call the fire department. In all seriousness, if the football legend JJ Watt can stay after a grueling 10-hour football practice for over an hour to sign autographs, you can stay for an extra 15 minutes after a three-hour show. If you think you're too famous or busy to greet "the public", you're just plain wrong. Again, it's part of your job as a performer.

Second, you should make sure to be kind, always positive, and never ever reveal important personal details about yourself OR any of your fellow performers. It's not cool if an autograph-seeker asks, "What is Lin Manuel Miranda's warm-up process?" and you answer anything other than, "You should tweet him and ask him!" or "I'm not sure. I'm always worried about my own warm-up". (Unless you, in fact, are Lin and then you can say whatever the heck you want). Never ever give someone on social media or at the stage door that you don't know your personal email, phone number, or address. Even if they're super cool and sweet and seemingly harmless, this can go really wrong really quickly. Don't think that dancers have creepy fans? Think again. I can name many. Protect yourself and your privacy WHILE you're being kind and generous. It's a fine line, but once you find it, you're set.

Agent's Take: It is not your responsibility to provide information on another person; let them speak for themselves. It is better to say less than regret overstepping your boundaries.

On a side note, loyal fans can be supportive, thoughtful, and just plain fun! When the ladies' dressing room of a particular show I was in happened to mention on social media that we love Trader Joe's cookie butter, a big box of it showed up at the stage door a week later. (Incidentally, our costumes were pretty tight for the next week or so). Additionally, I personally have a very kind and loyal fan who donated a thousand dollars to a short film for which I was raising money on a crowd funding site. And best of all, a thoughtful young lady that was the self-proclaimed president of the fan club of one of the roles that I understudied happens to work for Disney World and gives me free tickets for myself and my friends any time I want to go. In general, people aren't weird, they're just thankful for your hard work and for making them feel something. Dance in any genre can be life-changing for an audience member and as performers, we can sometimes forget that. If a person that has witnessed your artistry is thankful, don't be suspicious. Be grateful and acknowledge that you have been a small part of enriching the life of another human. And sign freaking autographs for goodness' sake.

- **Save your pennies** – You'll read more about financial planning in the next chapter, but every dancer MUST save some of their salary while working to assure financial security when they're not working. I was absolutely terrible about doing this and got myself into some pretty tough spots the first few years (okay, more than a few years) that I was performing. If you're a naturally positive or confident person, it's so easy to think, "I'll just pay off this credit card when I book another national commercial" or "This event is totally going to be great networking, an ideal red carpet opportunity, so buying this expensive dress is a great career move". My most popular excuse was, "My education is important and will pay off in the long run, so two voice lessons, two acting classes, one trapeze lesson, and six dance classes per week plus my monthly gym and Bikram yoga memberships are completely legitimate investments. Not to mention I can totally write them off". In hindsight, this was a completely ridiculous assumption and I paid dearly for it (a 22.9% APR to be exact). And, incidentally, if you write off too many classes, that's a total IRS red flag and audits are time consuming and expensive. Trust me, I've been through two of them!

Yes, it's great to be confident and positive about the future of your dance career, but wouldn't you rather go to Vegas for a weekend with your friends than pay off credit card debt when you get that surprise residual check? I would. So, SAVE your money. If it's a longer-term gig, I like to set up direct deposit into two different bank accounts. I set a percentage to go to my savings account and a percentage to go to my checking. Right now, I send 15 percent to my savings account per paycheck and I don't ever touch it or see it. I don't even look at the balance that often because it's very tempting to spend that dough. If it's a shorter-term gig, you'll have to send that money over to savings yourself, but make sure you do it as soon as possible. The longer that cheddar sits in your checking account, the more likely you are to use it for a new pair of leather pants (the pants which you'll have to sell six months later when you can't pay your rent). Ideally, you should have at least 3-6 months' worth of living expenses in a pot that you don't touch until you need it.

∼

AGENT'S TAKE: Make sure you start a separate savings account that is designated for joining the union. If you are not a member, the initial cost can be significant. Contribute to that sunny day fund so when you need to join, it is not a jolt to your bank account.

∼

- **Leverage your current work to get future work** – There is no better time to reconnect with all of the people on your networking spreadsheet than when you're working. If you're doing a live performance, the best time to connect with your contacts is a week or two before your performances start. If you're doing an on-camera gig, you should contact your folks a day or two before your work airs. Letting casting directors, choreographers, agents, managers, directors, and fellow dancers know that you're working is not, and I repeat, not bragging. This is the one time you can share your success and still be seen as gracious and appropriate. AND it's another point of contact (remember that from chapter 3?). The law of attraction, or "like attracts like" applies to working in the industry. It's a natural human reaction (even for casting folks) to be more likely to hire a dancer that has been hired by someone else. Many dancers swear on the importance of this momentum (and some have weird rituals to keep it). But, if you don't let your contacts know that you're working, they will more than likely not get the memo. And if a tree falls in the forest . . .

If you're still a little shy about spreading the good news, you can couch it in an opportunity, discount, or fun experience for your folks. First of all, if there happen to be any specific casting directors, agents, or choreographers that you want to impress (and you're doing something that shows you off and is a live performance), this is your opportunity to put your money where your mouth is. Offer your target person (or people) a free ticket to see you strut your stuff. The key here is to be nonchalant about the whole I'm-buying-you-a-ticket-so-you-will-see-I'm-awesome-and-sign/hire-me thing. Something like, "Hey! I'm doing such-and-such show and I think it will be a fun evening. I have an extra ticket if you're free. Let me know if you'd like to come", works wonders. Maybe your target person won't take you up on the ticket, but you've probably made them feel valued and you've definitely let them know that you're working.

For your fellow dancer pals and non-specifically-targeted industry professionals, there are a few options. If you have an on-camera appearance on television or a web appearance that has a specific release time, you can add a fun experience opportunity for contacts to watch it. "Check me out tomorrow night on Modern Family! I'll bet you can't find the extra that is an EXACT Carmen Elektra look-alike. I almost got a photo!". This puts forward your experience in a jovial light and also sets viewers up for a "Where's Waldo" experience. If you're doing a stage show and the company gives you any kind of discount code for friends and family, this is the perfect vehicle to reaching out to contacts. "Hi, friend! I'm doing this super sexy burlesque show next week. If you happen to want to come see us shake it, you can get 15% off your ticket with this code".

While you do want to spread the good news about your employment fortune, you definitely don't want to overdo it. A maximum of two social media posts before your event is more than sufficient. And remember to comply by any privacy specifications set forth by your producers – in other words, don't spill the beans before they should be spilt. The moral of the story is to be delicate with the feelings of your dancer friends who are currently unemployed or who may or may not have auditioned for the gig you're doing. Imagine yourself on the other side of your correspondence and if it's cool with you, it will probably be cool with everyone else.

AGENT'S TAKE: Keep in mind, those who are in the industry like to support the industry. Let people know of events and shows you are doing. It will give them the opportunity to support what you are doing, to see you do what you do best, and it validates your commitment to the industry.

- **Don't forget the people that made it happen** – If you have a fabulous job that you got through the help of an agent, manager, casting director, friend, family member, or acquaintance, please do not forget to show your gratitude. Thank the dancer that introduced you to the choreographer that hired you. Send a card to the manager that procured your audition appointment. Send a fun photo of you with your new cast mates to Sally casting director with a thank you note.

Trust me, a proper thank you goes a long way AND . . . you guessed it. It's another point of contact.

I tend to go a little overboard with my thank you acknowledgements. The scope of your expressions of gratitude is completely up to you, but I like to find out exactly what the person I'm thanking likes and send them a little gift. One of my agents happens to love flowers, coffee, and champagne. If she books me a great gig, I'll usually send a small one of these three along with a thank you card. There's no use in sending chocolate to your lactose-intolerant choreographer (in fact, it could be seen as insensitive), so please do your research. The best way is to just give a call to your intended recipient's assistant and just ask what they like. Remember, though, that if you get too extravagant with your note/gift, it can look super desperate. Unless you book a gig where you're making well over six figures, please don't spend all your dough on sending the casting director a bottle of Cristal.

Additionally, proper etiquette (or, at least, dancer etiquette in my book of manners) is to make sure that if you're doing a live performance and tickets are available, you arrange great seats for your representation. Take care of them first because they're probably the ones that got you the job. Sometimes your folks purchase their own seats and sometimes they already have them, but it is the right thing to do to make sure that they're taken care of in every way.

AGENT'S TAKE: Congrats. Now that you have booked a job, you have the opportunity to reflect how you can handle your business skills alongside of your creative skills. In addition to bringing your A-game to the production as an artist, you now need to bring those same skills to the business side. Did you read your agreement? Do you know what is expected of you? Do you know what production will provide and what they will not provide? Are you clear on your commitment to production? Are

you willing to be flexible and handle many different personalities under stressful situations?

As your career evolves into booking work, take your skills from dance class and apply your dedication, consistency, and attention to detail to the business side of your career. A well-rounded artist that handles their creative work and business smoothly is generally well respected and tends to work consistently in the industry.

~

To sum up this chapter on working in dance, I will say again that if you're a dancer and you're lucky enough to be paid to do the thing you love the most, you're absolutely winning at life. Never ever take any moment of working as a dancer for granted because there are hundreds of thousands of people around the world that would ecstatically take your place. Working as a dancer requires accepting a good amount of responsibility. If you're making a paycheck, it's your responsibility to work every minute of every rehearsal, performance, and shoot day to the best of your physical and mental ability. You also have a responsibility to contribute in a consistently positive manner to the atmosphere in the rehearsal room, backstage, onstage, on set, and in all social settings. Finally, you have a responsibility to yourself to make the most of your experience by taking care of your health and your safety, being mentally present and aware in every moment, and enjoying every second of your opportunity as if it were your last.

9

Thriving

There is a huge misconception that when a dancer gets a good job, they've "made it" and they'll never have to be unemployed again. There is also an equally-as-huge misconception that when a dancer achieves a certain level of status that they've "made it" and will never have to audition or be unemployed again. Guess what? No dancer, actor, entrepreneur, writer, or, well, anyone has ever "made it". No one gets to rest in the dance industry on any kind of laurels. And why would you want to, anyway? Dancing is fun, challenging, and (hopefully) artistically fulfilling – why would you want to stop?

Unfortunately, though, unemployment and breaks between gigs are inevitable. No matter how much fame or recognition you've achieved, you should be prepared to not only deal with unemployment, but to use it as a platform for even more success. I have heard dancers refer to unemployment as "funemployment" – I love that attitude and it's very necessary. You'd better learn to turn your lemons to lemonade because I don't know a single dancer (or actor, or singer, or any kind of artist) that has not had the PLEASURE of having down time between gigs. I know Tony award winners that have had long stretches of time off between gigs as well as long stretches of time before they even have a next gig. I repeat: Tony award winners. Time off in the dance industry is the norm and if you want to have a successful and long career, you'll take full advantage of your time off so that when you have a new opportunity, you're ready to face it head-on.

There are many productive things you can do for your career and your well being when you're not working in the dance industry. Some of these things are imperative to keeping your life and career on point and some are merely suggestions to further your career in the years to come. There are three things you should do that are absolutely imperative in maintaining your employability and your quality of life while you have time off. Here they are:

TAKE CARE OF YOUR FINANCES

There is a reason this chapter is titled "Thriving" rather than "Surviving" or even "Starving". The title is taken from a book that's written by two dear friends of mine called *The Thriving Artists: A Guide to an Inspired Life, Empowered Career, and Entrepreneurial Finances.* The authors, Joe and Christine Abraham, posit that we don't have to be starving artists in order to honor our craft and make it lucrative. We don't have to be starving artists; we can, in fact, thrive. In their book, Joe and Christine help you to release any fears about money, generate income, and effectively manage every penny you make. Why am I recommending a book rather than telling you how to take care of your finances yourself? Well, because I'm not quite an expert on that subject (see previous chapter's explanation). One of the wisest things a person can say is "I don't know". While I do have some good ideas about the personal finances of artists now that I'm (ahem) slightly more mature, I am in no way an expert. Thus the referral. Whether you read The Thriving Artists or not, I recommend learning in some way how to best handle and grow your finances.

When you choose to be a professional dancer, you inherently are choosing a freelance career. Even the more stable dancing jobs like dancing for ballet and modern companies and performing in Broadway shows are rarely stable. Broadway shows close with little to no notice and unless you're in one of the 3-5 long-running shows in New York or a national tour and you choose to stay, you're going to be looking for a new gig every 3-15 months. If you're in a dance company, even if you decide to be a lifer and stay with the company for a twenty-year stretch, most ballet and modern companies have lengthy periods during the season where dancers have unpaid time off (most prominent ballet companies run a 34-40-week season per 52-week year). Regardless of your chosen corner of the dance world, you will have to pay attention to your finances.

Let's take, for example, Freddie. Freddie is a tap dancer in Chicago that has been around the block a few times and has many connections in the industry. In January, he books a national commercial and his agent negotiates a total of approximately $2,000 for one shoot day and one day of rehearsal. Freddie then goes three weeks without booking a gig and then books an industrial for a large company that includes two weeks of work and five performances for which he's paid $1,200 per week and $400/performance. Not bad, Freddie! After that gig, though, he has a bit of a dry spell and books only two music videos in April for a tap company that pay $100/day (one shoot day and one rehearsal day per video). Freddie pounds the pavement and then lands an out-of-town summer stock musical theatre gig paying $550/week for six weeks in July and August. After Freddie gets back into town, he immediately starts auditioning and after two weeks, he books the role of Phil in a production of White Christmas in Texas that pays $650/week, but it doesn't start until mid-November and it's only five weeks long. He doesn't get any other work during the calendar year, but he does receive three fabulous residual checks from his national commercial in January that total $4,500 in the month of November.

Sounds like Freddie is a very successful tap dancer, yes? In one year, he has procured a total of six great dancing jobs and he's making as much as $1,000 per day. Yes, Freddie is winning, but if he had not been wise in January and saved his money, he would have been in a bit of trouble. Let's total up Freddie's annual dancing income. Including all rehearsal days, performance days, and residuals, Freddie has made a total of $17,850 in dancing income, which is just about $6,000 over the federal poverty level for 2016. Doesn't sound so lucrative anymore, does it? While this isn't the ideal financial situation for a professional dancer, it IS live-able if Freddie's smart about his finances, spreads out his income, and seeks out a few other sources of (hopefully dance-related) work.

The fact of the matter is, you should know exactly how much money you have coming in, exactly how much money you have going out, and exactly what additional resources you have available to you as a dancer. If Freddie files for unemployment after he leaves his summer gig, he's already garnered an extra $418/week in the state of Illinois for his 10 weeks of unemployment from September through mid-November. If he also asks around and finds a high school tap student that needs weekly coaching for her national tap competition, he can pull in an extra $75/week from January-May.

This has already added an extra $5,680 to Freddie's annual income and brought it up to $23,530. If he is wise and utilizes his (limited) resources, he has $450/week with which to live in Chicago.

Yes, of course, many famous dancers are paid wages well over six figures and that's great, but while our friend Freddie may be on the lower end of the earning spectrum of professional dancers, I've taken the time to detail this example to let you know that even if you're not famous, a dancing career is absolutely possible. Most dancers, when they're not performing, take on dance-adjacent gigs to supplement their dancing income while they're doing lower-paying dancing jobs or in between higher-paying dancing jobs. Check out the list of performance-adjacent jobs below, choose the one(s) that sound interesting to you, and have them in your back pocket. But first, learn how to take care of your finances and be a wise artist. Thriving is always much more fun than starving.

TAKE CARE OF YOURSELF

You've heard it a thousand times, but you'll hear it here again. Your body is your instrument, Please make the effort to take care of your instrument; your Stradivarious, your RED camera, your Italian horsehair paintbrush. Unfortunately for you and your potentially vibrant social life, you also happen to live inside your instrument. The first chair violinist at the New York Philharmonic, the Oscar-winning Director of Photography, and the artist that just landed an exhibit at the Guggenheim all work with materials outside their bodies. Yours IS your body. I know, this is still not news, but being a professional dancer can (and sometimes should) dictate some of the aspects of how you conduct your life. It's simple – if you care enough about your art and your dance career, you will make the effort to ensure that your everyday actions leave you in an optimal position to perform your craft to the best of your abilities.

The most successful dancers make sure that they get 8-10 hours of sleep per night so their muscles can recoup from their days of rigorous physical work. This may mean that you have to bow out of a social event a little early or forego binge watching that fifth season of House of Cards. According to the US national library of medicine, moderate sleep deprivation produces impairments in cognitive and motor performance equivalent to legally prescribed levels of alcohol intoxication (www.ncbi.nlm.nih.gov). In other words, if you stay out and party like it's 1999 (anybody remember that song?), you basically show up at rehearsal the next day as much as wasted. All-nighters are scientifically proven to be the equivalent of worse than a half a bottle of wine with breakfast. If you wouldn't dare do that, reconsider your sleep habits. If you would, well, that's a whole other story and you should maybe seek a little outside help.

The worst injury of my career was the direct product of sleep deprivation. I was working on a Broadway show and had decided to pick up a bit of extra money doing personal training on the side. Unfortunately, one of my clients scheduled 6am workout sessions . . . in Brooklyn. Since I was living in New Jersey at the time (incidentally, Weehawken is an excellent, affordable, and safe option for any dancers looking for a place to live in the New York area), I had to wake up at 4:45am three times per week to meet my enthusiastic client. Since my show came down at 10:45pm, I rarely got home before midnight. That equals (on a good day) 4-5 hours of sleep per night. One particular morning, I had a 9am invited call audition for the show Memphis. I grabbed a large coffee after my 6am training session and went straight for my audition. While in the audition, I made a (probably poor) decision to chassé into what I hoped to be a triple attitude turn. My right standing leg slipped out from under myself, I caught air while my left leg was going into attitude, and my entire body landed on my backward left ankle. Because of my lack of sleep and motor skills, I didn't have the wherewithal to tuck my back leg back under me to minimize the impact. It was one of those moments where everyone gasps, the music stops, and the world stops. The lovely choreographer's assistant carried me to the side of the room, gave me some ice, and I had a fabulously broken talus bone that would render me a "singer" (rather than a dancer) on Broadway for the next two years.

Agent's Take: Take care of yourself. Give yourself plenty of rest, healthy food, ample water, and time to recuperate. You

cannot expect your body to perform well when you are not being respectful of yourself. Dancers put themselves through grueling amounts of class and training; make sure you are being diligent in providing a healthy environment for your mind and body so it can reward you when you need to perform.

One of the best pieces of advice I received was to set an alarm to GO to bed. Most of us set an alarm to wake up, but we seem to have so much time at the end of the night and an extra ten minutes of hanging out on social media or watching television turns into an hour or two of lost sleep. That then turns into an (estimated) 10% less focused day of rehearsal, show, or audition. Sometimes 10% is the difference between you and another dancer. Just go to sleep. If you need a little extra scientific evidence for the importance of getting your Z's, I recommend Arianna Huffington's book Thrive. Maybe read it as you go to sleep . . .

Another thing - successful dancers EAT. Dancers are athletes. End of story. Can you imagine an Olympic sprinter deciding to not eat for a day or so before her race so she looks "super skinny"? No. Food is fuel and if you're in Boston Ballet, basically the human version of a Mercedes AMG, your badass car needs some seriously premium fuel. Human premium fuel equals whole foods, protein, vegetables, and all that stuff that you all read about in the magazines and Michael Pollen books. If you don't put fuel into your body on a regular basis, your Mercedes AMG ends up gas-less by the side of the 405 while the hybrid passes you by. Do not ever let yourself perform at less than the peak of your potential because you have been irresponsible with what you have put (or not put) in your mouth.

On the flip side of the coin, I have seen many a dancer lose a job because they were seen as "not fit enough" by the folks behind the table. You are born with the genes you are born with and you can't change that. However, you can work it to the best of your abilities. If you happen to be on the chunkier side, get the heck in the gym and make those chunks muscles. (Incidentally, I'd like to personally thank Beyoncé for leading the charge in making curvy women popular in the music video culture and Darcey Bussell, for making women with curves palatable in the ballet world. You are female pioneers and young dancers throughout the world thank you!).

BUT just because curves are in, this does not give you the excuse to cancel your gym membership. Cross training is so, so crucial in the dance world. If you're a male commercial dancer, you'd better be doing some serious push ups and bicep curls to tone your shirtless bod to look fierce next to Britney in her new Vegas show. If you're a female musical theatre chorine and you want to rock it out as a Radio City Rockette, you'd better schedule some Pilates sessions to lengthen those svelte gams for Thanksgiving Day Parade close-up goodness. There is absolutely no excuse for not cross-training as a dancer. If you don't belong to a gym or have a personal trainer, there are thousands of instructional videos online. If you're afraid that you'll get "bulky", you won't. I guarantee it. If you cross train and you get too "bulky" for your dance career and you can prove it, then I'm a monkey's uncle (Lion King reference, anyone?). It very, very rarely happens. If you're worried about gaining too much muscle mass, refrain from protein drinks or performance enhancers and work out using your own body weight instead of heavy dumbbells.

Agent's Take: Don't forget to hydrate. Water is just as essential as food is to fuel your body. Drink up – stay hydrated.

Additionally, and I would love to not have to include this point, but inappropriate use of prescription or illegal substances and/or drinking alcohol in excess is the worst thing you can do for your dance career. And smoking cigarettes stopped being cool a good ten years ago. First of all, a glass of wine is about 120-140 calories and if you have three, that is the equivalent of a good meal of "fuel". If you consume 3 glasses of wine three times per week in a month, that's an extra 1.2 pounds of FAT that you gain. Per month. I'm not condoning abstinence by any stretch of the imagination, but moderation is everything. A glass of wine with coworkers is great for your social game and it's healthy and full of antioxidants. If you get plastered and do something stupid and/or illegal while under the influence, you could get fired, black balled, or arrested. I don't know many well-known music artists that want to hire dancers with criminal records for their next world tour.

AGENT'S TAKE: When your body is sore from class, rehearsal, or all of the above, it is easy to find ease in substances. If you are of age to drink, a nice glass of wine can ease those aches a bit. However, you should simply do so in moderation. Do not allow a substance to sabotage all the work you have put into your career. You have invested too much in training and commitment to your success to put a huge block in the road by abusing any substances.

The moral of the story is that you should treat yourself and your body with the same care and consideration that you would another human. Sometimes dancers tend to think that they can overcome anything with their steadfast and well-practiced willpower. Sometimes we think we're superheroes. We go to ballet class, rehearsal, do a show, and catch a midnight yoga class to get a leg up on the competition. There is a line, though, between pushing ourselves just enough and too much. Actually, it's not a line. It's a very steep cliff. I urge you all to keep a safe distance from that cliff because once you go over, it's sometimes impossible to climb back up. Taking as many dance classes as possible is only effective if you are healthy and present enough to be 100% in the room and at the top of your game while taking them. You can get more from one focused hour in a good class than three hours where you're simply going through the motions. In the great words of Steve Jobs, "Quality is more important than quantity. One home run is much better than two doubles". Be wise about being kind to yourself.

TAKE CARE OF YOUR ART

If you happen to have some time where you are not being paid to work as a dancer, you absolutely should not stop dancing. The old adage is, "If you miss one day of class, no one notices; if you miss two days of class, you notice; if you miss three days, everyone notices". Artistic freedom in dance is most often found through technique. You cannot go wrong if you spend your down time in a studio perfecting your technique. Well, hopefully you'll be perfecting your techniques (with an S) because if you're a savvy dancer, you're well-versed in many styles of dance. Don't have the dough to pay for a lot of expensive dance classes? Gather a few of your dancing buddies and agree to teach each other your moves. You'll be surprised how much you can learn from your fellow dancers. If you all don't have the money to pool to rent an empty dance studio, move some furniture in someone's living room and BYO full-length back-of-door mirror. When there's a will, there's a way. And I guarantee you that if you start a free dance class group, ever how makeshift it is, you'll be one of the more popular kids on the playground. This may also give you the opportunity to stretch your choreographic muscles and set some of your moves on your friends. You could even put some of your choreography on social media if it's good. The point is that you should never have an excuse for not learning, improving, and dancing. Ever. Until you're dead.

There are so many ways to use your down time to take care of your art. Read plays, watch films, and see performances. The more educated you are on other forms of art, the more rich your future performances will become. You'll be surprised how many of these things performances and resources are (or can be) super cheap or free. If they're not free, you can offer up your time in exchange. Many dance festivals will give you free tickets if you volunteer to usher. Yoga studios offer work-study programs in exchange for free classes. Steps in NYC and Millennium in Los Angeles have great work-study programs that give you free or discounted classes in exchange for things like working the front desk or cleaning studios. This also helps you to use your down time to widen your connection net. If you're working at a dance studio, you'll inevitably meet teachers and choreographers. If you volunteer for a dance-related charity performance, you'll meet tons of people that are either in the industry or related to the industry. Say hi and make a genuine connection. If you're between gigs, you probably will have even more time to spend getting to know them. Remember that when you're not working as a dancer, your time is a huge resource. Use it to expand your mind, strengthen your body, and prepare for the inevitable great job that is in your future.

∼

Agent's Take: Keeping a positive and level perspective is essential. There will be ups and downs within your career, therefore stay focused and find a core group of industry-related friends that you can connect with. No one will better understand all you are going through than those who are perusing likeminded aspirations. Connecting to our industry community will provide support, guidance and inspiration on a consistent basis. The industry can be overwhelming; therefore having a group that supports one another's goals as artists will bring balance and peace along your path to success.

∼

Chances are, if you're not being paid to dance for an amount of time, you probably want to find a part-time gig to pay the bills (and to pay for your class card at Millennium). I fully support a part-time job, but I think that the forward-thinking dancer chooses their extra work wisely. The ideal down-time job both creates immediate revenue as well as sets a dancer up for a long-term career in a dance-adjacent field after their performance days have come to an end (more about this in chapter 10). According to research by the Bureau of Labor Statistics, a person graduating from high school in 2015 will hold an average of 12-15 jobs in a lifetime. Guess what? Not all of those jobs have to be in the same field! The skills that you garner from spending a lifetime training in dance are an ideal base for many jobs and careers outside of the realm of auditioning and performing.

So, while you have some down time, why not spend a little of that time educating yourself and gaining work experience in a field that may or may not eventually become your full-time job? The list of employers that would love to hire a disciplined, fit, intelligent dancer on a part-time basis are endless. Here are a few great part-time dance-adjacent and usually very-flexible jobs to check out while you're not on tour with Britney or dancing The Nutcracker at the Met:

Teaching dance – Find a local dance school and start by cutting your teeth on the little kids (weird horror film analogy acknowledged). Then move up the age ranks from there and find what age dance student with which you best connect. You might find it fun to teach three-year-olds to chassé or you might love breaking down a fouetté for high school freshmen. Many dance schools love to hire working dancers because you bring street cred to their faculty! And generally, if you're a currently working dancer, you can bring industry insight to their older dancers that may be soon entering it themselves. Teaching pays a great hourly rate and it's generally pretty easy to find a sub if you have a last-minute audition that comes up.

AGENT'S TAKE: Give back to the industry by sharing your knowledge. Teaching can be a wonderful way to share your insight, advice and educate the next generation of artists. Many artists are exceptional educators, especially when they apply teaching skills that enhance a dancer's vocabulary, technical ability, stage presence and injury prevention. Being a mentor and educator to artists can be fulfilling, especially with the wide range of teaching positions that are available.

Personal Training – This one takes a little work to get started, but you'll be surprised how much, as a dancer, you already know about the human body! In order to become a personal trainer, you generally need to obtain a certification from a reputable certification program. The NCCA (National Commission for Certifying Agencies) recognizes about 15 different personal training certification programs and some of them can be done online in your own time! I studied for, completed, and received my certification from the National Academy of Sports Medicine in six months backstage while I was swinging a Broadway show. Once you have your certification, you can choose to work at a gym or go it your own with private training. Both are great ways to keep in shape, make extra money, and keep your schedule very flexible. If you happen to book a music video, you can just call up your client and reschedule their sweat session. Many prospective clients love the status of working out with a real professional dancer!

Choreography – If you happen to have a knack for choreography, there are many dance schools that hire outside choreographers to create their dance pieces. This is particularly prevalent in dance schools that attend competitions and can be a super fun way to get your creative on and inspire the generations of the future!

AGENT'S TAKE: Setting routines on dancers for competition is a terrific way to connect with young performers as well as hone your choreographic style of work. Staying fresh with your choreography is essential and setting routines can be a good option for artists that are interested in working with young dancers.

Group Fitness Classes – This is a great option for dancers that don't necessarily enjoy instructing younger humans but who like to inspire others. Hundreds of new group fitness classes are popping up around the globe and they're all clamoring for dancers to teach them. Ballet barre workout classes, Latin dance classes, Pilates, pole dancing classes, yoga classes, hip hop workout classes, you name it. The dance class workout craze is alive and booming. You may have to obtain a certification or training to teach these classes, but once you do, you have a great new very-employable skill. Some workout studios like Physique 57 actually pay you to learn their technique (if you're a dancer and looking for a little Rockette-inspired muscle lengthening, I highly recommend taking these classes as well). Additionally, if you're a dancer that's auditioning or in a show in the evening, many of these dance fitness class schedules are tailored around 9-to-5-ers so the main commitment is 6am-9am (before auditions or rehearsals) and 5pm-7pm (after auditions and before 7:30 half hour call).

Blogging/Writing – If you happen to have the literary gift of gab, there are opportunities for freelance writers that know things about dance. Numerous dance publications and websites look for dancers with good writing skills to see shows and review them or write articles for magazines. You can also consider starting your own dance-related blog. The adage "write what you know" is absolutely right! You may have some valuable insight into dance technique or the industry that many people want to read about! If your blog is successful enough, you'll hopefully find a sponsor or two. Worst-case scenario, you increase your positive presence on the web. **Note: Never ever reveal any information that is sensitive, personal, or negative on a blog or article. Keep it positive, relatable, and fun.

Conventions/Competitions – There are hundreds of dance competitions throughout the world that provide inspiration, education, and just plain fun to up-and-coming dancers. If you can nab a job teaching, judging, or even working behind the scenes for one of these, it's a fabulous way to meet people, do a little traveling, and lay the groundwork for a future post-performance career. Particularly if you have been on a dance television show, a Broadway show, or have other recognizable credits, this is a fun and flexible part-time gig to supplement your dancing career. Competitions and conventions are also generally held from Friday-Sunday or Monday morning, so it's not very likely that they would interfere with any auditions that might arise.

∼

AGENT'S TAKE: The dance convention and competition arena can be tremendous for an artist that has a true passion to teach. Teaching on a convention can be consistent work and (at times) provide flexible terms for an artist whose mainstay focus is performing/choreographing for film, television and live stage

show performances.

~

These are just a few examples of dance-adjacent part-time jobs that may pan out to eventually be your full-time career. Remember, though, that they don't have to be. A part-time job can be a part-time job, but why not keep yourself open to possibilities of future employment?

Lastly, keep in mind that having time off for dancers is absolutely the norm. You should never feel embarrassed or like you're not a talented dancer just because you are currently unemployed. Everyone understands this situation (and has more than likely experienced it) and the more you attempt to deny it or try to sugar-coat it, the less attractive you become. "I'm just auditioning right now and taking some fun new classes" is much more relatable than, "I just finished doing the movement workshop of that new musical and I was so exhausted that I'm taking a little time off" (particularly if that movement workshop was more than a week or two ago). People read right through that kind of thing, trust me. Perhaps if we're all completely transparent about our situations, we'll give another person the confidence to be transparent about their situation and then we can all just tell the unabashed truth to each other for once!

~

AGENT'S TAKE: Many other professions do not understand the inconsistency within the arts. Therefore, make sure to have a strong support team that is part of the industry as they can guide and keep you focused - - they understand the volatility of the business, have experienced the industry and can support you in your pursuits.

~

Remember that when you're choosing what to do with your time off from employed dancing, you should be actively making a choice. The worst thing you can do with down-time is to let it pass without making an effort to further your connections, your intelligence, and your art. Time is one of the human race's most important assets – don't waste a single bit.

∼

AGENT'S TAKE: Remember, every artist will take a different path and have a varied result in their career. This is what makes the industry so creative, unique and ever evolving. Not everyone has the ability to be a part of this incredible industry; be thankful you have a gift that allows you to be creative and pursue areas that few have the courage to dream of.

∼

10

Transitioning

The inevitable fact that every dancer must face is that there will more than likely be a time when your body starts to break down. Injuries, arthritis, loss of flexibility, and the breakdown of various parts of the body are all a part of the cycle of human life. Dance performance careers are often very short in comparison to the average career. If a dancer is lucky, healthy, and takes good care of their body, they can expect a good 20-25 years of dancing after school before they need to close up shop and only dance for fun. Obviously, there are fabulous and famous exceptions to this generalization. I just read an article about an 82-year-old burlesque dancer who is still shaking her tassels and Mikhail Baryshnikov is still on stage at 65. Wendy Whelan retired from New York City Ballet at 48 to start her contemporary dance career and Merce Cunningham performed well into his 60's.

On the other side of the coin, according to a study in Australia, Switzerland, the US, and other countries, the average dancer stops dancing professionally in their early to mid-thirties. If you ask most professional dancers, they'll tell you that they are well aware of this fact. Unfortunately, though, most of those dancers are ill-prepared when this time comes to move on to a new (and potentially equally as fulfilling) career. Whether it's denial, blinders, or laser focus, thousands of dancers leave "the industry" every year without specific plans for the future. In the always-beautiful words of the eloquent Martha Graham, "A dancer dies twice—once when they stop dancing, and this first death is the more painful."

First of all, let's play a game. Set a timer for five minutes and write down as many post-performance careers as you can think of. Ready? Set? Go!

You probably thought first of dance teacher, choreographer, and Pilates instructor. Great. Here are a few others:

Dance teacher
Choreographer (companies, music artists, commercials)
Director
College dance professor
Stage manager
Ballet master/mistress
Set designer
Dance therapist
Dance photographer
Group fitness instructor
Massage therapist
Personal trainer
Dance costume designer
Dance notation
Wig designer/hair stylist
Dance agent or manager
Yoga/Pilates teacher
Dance writer/blogger
Physical therapist
Arts administration
Artistic director
Private dance instructor (weddings, events)
Makeup artist
Actor
Dance competition owner/judge
Videographer/filmmaker
Arts fundraiser
Public relations for arts companies
Tour manager
Dance critic
Lighting designer
Production manager
Stage hand
Theatre ticket sales
Special events planner for arts organizations
Social media coordinator for a dance company

And those are just the careers that are related to dance!

Dancers generally do a really great job in almost any career because we're dedicated, focused, and not averse to hard work. The sky is the limit for what you can do after a performing career and in my opinion, it should be more of a rebirth than a death (all due respect to the late Ms. Graham).

If you are a dancer that is looking to transition into a different career and you have a good number of years of professional experience, Career Transition for Dancers offers scholarships and grants that will go toward furthering your education and helping you gain the skills and materials to thrive after (or while) dancing. In 2011, I decided that I wanted to start branching off into the field of personal training – in fact, I had a dream to start my own personal training business. I was working as a swing in a show at the time (I'm sure you know, but a swing is basically an understudy for the entire ensemble of a show, so swings have a lot of pressure) and I had a lot of down time. I applied to Career Transition for Dancers for help with creating my new personal training business and a short time later, they had paid for my National Academy of Sports Medicine certification, my workout equipment, the software to design my own website, and a few other super-useful things to start my own business. And guess what? I did! Thanks to CTFD, I was able to educate myself while performing and now I have an entire skill set (and a significant amount of experience since 2011) with which to build an alternative career.

The key to transition is education. The earlier you can start your education, the better. Rather than celebrating your retirement from the stage and then enrolling in, say, massage therapy school, why not gather your massage therapy skills in evening classes while you can still pay the bills dancing? Additionally, dancers shouldn't feel as if they have to only choose one educational path. While education in some fields can be time-consuming and pricey, double the education means double the employability. If you were a client, wouldn't you rather hire a massage therapist that is also a certified yoga instructor and personal trainer rather than just a massage therapist? And wouldn't you think that if a massage therapist had such a large skill set, don't you think that massage therapist might be able to charge more for his or her services? I think they could. While education costs, it generally pays off in spades in the long run.

Many dancers believe that the end of their performing career has to be abrupt; a hard and straight line on the timeline of their lives. "In 2015 I was a dancer and in 2016 I was a photographer". This is rarely the case and definitely not necessary. I've seen ballet dancers spend years transitioning; working their new career in the spring, summer, and fall and picking up a Nutcracker gig or two in the winter. The same goes for musical theatre dancers. Even I am not opposed to picking up a theatre or musical theatre gig every now and then if I have the time. It's fun and it's rejuvenating. If a friend calls and says (true story), "I need some hot chick dancers that can do martial arts for a music video I'm shooting in Pasadena tomorrow. Wanna come play?". If you are healthy and have time, the answer should always be "YES". Once you're a dancer, you'll always be a dancer even when it's not your primary source of income or the thing at which you now spend the majority of your time.

If you are thinking of transitioning and/or cutting back on the amount or type of dance jobs you would like to pursue, please let your agent(s) and manager(s) know as soon as possible. Similarly, if you're battling an injury, they need to know this information as well. More information disclosure with your representation is always better than less. If, for instance, you have a shoulder injury, your representation should know so that he or she don't submit you for a gig that involves heavy partnering. This doesn't mean that you'll be cut out of every audition, though! If there happens to be a great tap music video audition for Syncopated Ladies (I LOVE them, by the way!), you might be able to attend.

Likewise, if you are actively pursuing a career in arts administration and only want to do shorter-term gigs like television, commercials, or videos, you need to tell your representation. If you don't tell them, they spend a significant amount of their precious time pitching you for a tour with a music artist, and then they call with your audition only to have you turn it down . . . that's just bad business. Be transparent. You can always change your mind, decide to be full-out back in the industry, make a call to let your folks know, and you're back on the scene. Very few things in the dance industry are reversible if you remain consistently open and honest.

Choosing the right way to transition out of the industry is a very personal ordeal. Some dancers leave with a chip on their shoulder and begrudging the fact that they didn't have more years of dancing. If that's you, get the heck out. Choose a non-dance-related career and shut down your social media. Do not poison the delicate and vulnerable lives of those who are still cutting a rug with your ickiness. If you're a content and optimistic transitioner, kick around the idea of teaching or trying your hand at choreography (just don't kick too high). The more positive influences in the dance world, the more creative and supportive it will become and if you feel you can contribute to making the industry better from the other side of the performance space, I highly encourage you to do exactly that.

∼

AGENTS TAKE: One of the most exciting (and at times frightening) times is when artists grow into an added phase of their career. Industry experience can lead artists into new areas in which to flourish, whether it is in production, directing, producing or educating. The industry is always changing, therefore so will your career. Keep a keen eye on the areas that you are drawn to; make connections in those areas and support the projects to which you can attach yourself. You never know what the future holds, how the industry will shift, or who may be able to offer you a position in an area that you never expected.

Many artists feel that transitioning is limiting; that is looking at a glass half full. The reality is there are so many more opportunities to be perused due to the amount of experience and education an artist has to offer. And, the areas are unlimited since this applies to all industry related projects in front and behind the camera (ie film, television, commercial, digital, live stage show, education based, etc.)

With the vast knowledge and skill that an artist has obtained, many can seamlessly integrate into the business end of the industry as well. Keep in mind that many agents, managers,

entertainment attorneys, and studio executive were once working artists. Dedicating yourself to the industry allows an artist to grow within all stages of their career and provides savvy professionals to guide the next generation of aspiring talent.

Afterword

It is truly a gift to be drawn to the arts. Whether you are a dancer, actor or specialty artist, you have been granted the ability to tap into the creative realm. As you have read throughout this book, there are many areas within the industry. With the tremendous diversity and options available within the arts, there is more than enough space for every artist to find their creative area. There truly is no better time than the present to be a part of the dance industry. With the ever evolving digital, stage, and film platforms, the industry has more opportunity than ever to suit every artist's desires.

Remember to invest in yourself. Take the time to research, educate and discipline yourself for the goals you seek. You are the captain of your career, and it is your responsibility to set a course that is best suited for the skills that are uniquely honed to your abilities.

Connect to your industry community. Support the events and programs within the arts. This not only builds connections, it also will enhance and broaden your knowledge base. Be an active participant in your career, as well as to those who have the same dedication to dance and the Arts. How lucky it is to call yourself a dancer, and better yet to have a dance "family" that understands your commitment to this incredible industry.

Find balance in yourself, literally. There is an ebb and flow to your career. Give it time - allow yourself to find peace and understanding during the times you are pushing your technique to new levels. Make sure you are providing yourself realistic time to recuperate, rejuvenate and finding time to enjoy the gift you hold within you.

Unless you are a dancer, it is very difficult to explain the passion, drive and dedication you have for your love of dance. The true love of dance has an unspoken language within the industry. Those who share this gift within the industry truly know what an honor it is to call themselves *a dancer*. Now, get out there and make your dreams come true.

-Shelli Margheritis

If you've read this book, you probably love to dance. Or you're somebody that loves somebody that loves to dance. I believe that if this is true, dancing is in your bones and if you love it, you should do it, whether on a professional level, on a recreational level. Or on some level in between. Dancers should consider themselves part of the interwoven history of thousands of years and thousands of cultures. Dancing, in its many forms, is and has been an integral part of practically every civilization throughout the world (and probably the universe) because of its ability to entertain, surprise, inspire, and incite change in its participants and its viewers.

This book talks a lot about the nuts and bolts of the industry, what tactics to use to further your career, and ideas for integrating into the professional dance world. While all of those things are important, I urge you to never forget or neglect the joy in the artistry of dance. (I'm pretty sure that's why you fell in love with dancing in the first place.) Yes, dancing is a business, but it's also an art. It's an art in which you get to physically BE the art, to completely be immersed in its creation. Dance as an art is the perfect connection between music, space, and humans that has overtones with the power to travel straight to the heart.

Yes, the business of business of dance is important and making a living doing what you love is probably at the top of your list of things you want to do. If so, that's a great goal. You cannot, however, sacrifice any of the passion for dance that probably brought you into the industry in the first place. I have seen more than a few dancers become so engulfed in the love of the money, power, and fame brought by their success in the dance industry that they forgot about the love of the actual dancing. This brings about a bitterness and lack of collaboration that can be a rotten apple to any company of performers. Please, pretty please, don't let this kind of thing happen to you. Dancing is a privilege that so many people are unable to have and taking it for granted is just plain disrespectful. Enjoy the process, immerse yourself in the story, and enjoy the company and artistry of your fellow performers. This simple joy and appreciation for the power of the art will get your more jobs than any industry hack in the world.

Good dancing is one of the closest things on earth to having a super power. Dancers have the power to make another person feel something through their art, the power to make a person cry, the power to make a person laugh, the power to inspire romanticism, or the power to change another human's view of the world. Even more so than politicians and world leaders, artists have the ability, the visibility, and the responsibility to make a mark on their world; to use their movement to reshape the conceptions and misconceptions of their audience. If you consider yourself a dancer, take this conclusion as a challenge to do your duty to change the world for the better with the gift you've been given. Go out and use your dance to change the world.

--- Michelle Loucadoux

Acknowledgments

We would like to thank the following people for their expertise and support throughout the creation of this book. Front Cover Photographer: Vince Trupsin; Cover design: Leo Postovoit; Stylist: Ambrose Respicio; Hair/Make-up: Kimi Messina; Michelle's headshot photographer: Ray Garcia; Shelli's headshot photographer: Louise Flores; Michelle's favorite teacher: Arnott Mader; Advice and inspiration: Erin Bomboy; Patience and encouragement: Patrick Fraser; Everything: Kay and Dan Lookadoo; Shelli's better half: Marcel Margheritis, Support and street cred: MSA Agency; and last but not least: Relativity School and Glenn Kalison for introducing Shelli and Michelle.

MICHELLE LOUCADOUX has been a professional dancer and educator for over twenty years. Her experience spans from dancing with the Richmond Ballet and New Jersey Ballet to originating the Broadway casts of *Mary Poppins* and *The Little Mermaid* to dancing alongside well-known music artists on the large and small screen. Michelle has traveled the globe performing as well as training the next generation of performing artists. She is currently the program director of the commercial dance and contemporary musical theatre + film departments at Relativity School in Los Angeles.

With an extensive background spanning over 35 years as a professional dancer, author of *Making The Move* and *Brain Snacks*, keynote speaker and business entrepreneur, SHELLI MARGHERITIS brings a vast range of experience as an agent representing dancers, choreographers and educators for over ten years. As the first agent in history to develop a teaching division within a talent agency, she is the Director of Education and Choreography Agent at McDonald Selznick Associates (MSA) agency that represents world renowned talent for feature film, television, music videos, tours, Broadway shows, corporate events, Las Vegas spectaculars, commercials, as well as national and international dance education conventions. Shelli co-wrote the Commercial Dance BFA curriculum and is an active member of the advisory board for Relativity School. She is a proud member of the Television Academy and advocate within the dance industry.

ISBN 9780998605500

Printed in Great Britain
by Amazon